The Orphaned Adult

THE
ORPHANED
ADULT

*Understanding and Coping
with Grief and Change
After the Death of Our Parents*

Alexander Levy

PERSEUS BOOKS

Reading, Massachusetts

Copyright © 1999 by Alexander Levy

Perseus Books is a member of the Perseus Books Group.

Library of Congress Catalog Card Number: 99-64773
ISBN 0-7382-0099-9

Jacket design by Bruce W. Bond
Text design by Heather Hutchison
Set in 11-point Minion

2 3 4 5 6 7 8 9 10—03 02 01 00 99
First printing, July 1999

Perseus Books are available at special discounts for bulk purchases in the U.S. by corporations, institutions, and other organizations. For more information, please contact the Special Markets Department at HarperCollins Publishers, 10 East 53rd Street, New York, NY 10022, or call 1-212-207-7528.

Find us on the World Wide Web at http://www.perseusbooks.com

In loving memory of Saul and Elizabeth Levy

CONTENTS

ACKNOWLEDGMENTS

After my parents died, I began to think, "Someone ought to write a book about this experience." I even started believing I could write it. I started talking to others who had lost parents, did some research in the library, made notes, even wrote a few pages here and there—but write a book?

Believing in something, I learned, is a far cry from getting it done.

All that started to change when I met Colleen Mohyde, of the Doe Coover Agency in Boston, who took these ideas seriously and became their enthusiastic advocate. She introduced me to Marnie Cochran, senior editor at Perseus Books, and the opportunity for *The Orphaned Adult* was realized. Marnie was its champion.

Jeanne Marie Laskas, in addition to being my friend, companion, and wife, became my teacher. She read each chapter as I wrote it, patiently showing me where I was going astray or evading a difficult issue. She consistently held my writing up to the same standard she has for her own: It had to be beautiful and it had to be true. This book contains much of her.

From beginning to end, I was continuously cheered on by my loving family—all of them: Levys, Laskases, Martins, Caltabianos, and Karles. I am especially grateful to my children, Amy and Peter, gracious young adults who endured the formidable burden of having their father writing and talking about a subject they probably would rather not have been hearing and thinking about, at all.

Over 150 writers responded when I requested poetry and other writing pertinent to parental loss from the readers of *Poets and Writers* and *Writer's Journal* magazines. The poems eventually selected, which epitomize the original submissions, echo sentiments typically expressed more prosaically by us all.

And finally, none of this would have happened were it not for the generosity of friends, colleagues, and clients who shared their stories with me.

Thank you all.

The Orphaned Adult

Widowed Fathers

All they want is for you to be
the daughter that you might have been
if this were 1942,
to stay in the black-and-white house
and come softly down the shadowy stairwell
to sit on the couch with them, and watch the silence.

Dad, *you say,* please,
and you want to give them the world,
show them it's not so bad, good things to eat
in it, and shared music, maybe some live
entertainment, schmaltzy and outdated.

But they say no, thank you,
no world, *and they do*
the same thing every day,
go get the newspaper, and feed the cat,
resenting the way it rubs against their ankles
the way it did your mother's,
the same supper every day with the evening news.

You send them tea from England,
cookies from Norway,
you find these things unopened
when you come for Christmas
on the pantry shelves,
I was saving them, *they say*
embarrassedly, *for you*

Then they die, and there you are,
standing empty-handed,
your past snipped clean off,
the cat to feed.

—Janet McCann
College Station, TX

Here We Go
Loop-de-Loop

The Journey into the Unknown

Twice a year, once in the spring and once in the fall, on the anniversaries of my parents' deaths, I travel to the cemetery on the other side of town. Once there, I kneel beside the carved stone beneath which lie their remains, and I tend to the few small plants growing there.

The actual gardening requirements of a six-foot-square patch of real estate are modest: a bit of weeding, sweeping away some leaves that blew there from a nearby tree, and crushing a few clods of dirt back into the soil. I work with bare hands, smelling the earth and feeling the moist ground on my fingers and knees. I hear traffic passing on the road beyond the cemetery fence. Out of the corner of my eye, I see hillsides covered with other stone markers.

I don't go there to garden. I don't go there to visit my parents, either. There's nothing of them there. In fact, there's nothing of them anywhere at all. Maybe that's why I go to that spot, which, like me, carries their name. It is a place I go to spend time with memories. I'll sit for a while and wonder about many things, especially about the strange experience of having become an orphan as an adult.

I have only one vivid memory of the day my father died. I hold it in my mind like a black-and-white snapshot in which I am standing beside my car, staring at the green plastic bag containing his things that a nurse had handed me as I was leaving the hospital. I'm not moving in this picture. I am just standing there, staring. No sound. No odors. No sensations. No comprehension.

My father died in 1980, at the age of eighty-two, days after being operated on for a newly discovered malignant intestinal obstruction. There having been only six days between his diagnosis and his death, I struggled to find some meaning in my rapid transformation from a man with a father who was slow moving and alert to a man with a gaunt and disoriented father to a man with a wasted and comatose father to a man with no father at all.

Soon after his body was taken away, as I was standing in his suddenly very empty hospital room, I asked his doctor why an operation had been attempted on someone as old and weak as my father had been. This doctor, who had tended to our family for many years, rested his hand lightly on my arm, looked me directly in the eye, and, with an earnest tone and straight face, said, "We had to operate on him. Don't you understand? Your father wouldn't have lived a week if we hadn't."

I didn't know it yet, but this conversation was a harbinger of the surreal time of life I was entering: a time of transition from always having had two parents to, ultimately, forever having none.

On the day we buried my father's remains, I was uncertain whether my mother understood that he had died. Earlier that year she had abruptly become forgetful and confused, and by the time my father died, she was quite demented. Sitting down with me in her living room after we returned from the cemetery, she smiled sweetly and began looking around, her head slowly bobbing as though keeping time to a song only she could hear. In a tiny voice, she asked no one in particular, "Haven't they done a lovely job of decorating?"

It was like visiting a strange place with a stranger. Perhaps in an attempt to summon her back, I teased, "Oh come on, Mom. Do you mean to tell me that on top of everything else, you are starting to have problems with your memory?"

Her head became still, and she turned toward me. For the first time in months, and the last time ever, her eyes were focused and clear. In the thick Russian accent I knew so well, she said, "Yes. And I'm so sorry, but I'd like to stay that way."

She smiled fondly as her eyes began to fill with tears. Her head resumed its bobbing and then slowly began turning from side to side. Gradually her eyes defocused, became dry, and, once again, she was a stranger.

Always a woman of her word, she did stay that way, although probably not so much because of any decision she had made, until she began to get worse. Over the next four years, she grew increasingly frail and senile. By the end of her life, in 1984, she was one of those crazy old ladies about whom she had always said with a shudder, "I hope I never become like that."

On the day I buried her, the by-now-familiar cemetery hillside of flowers, stone, and grass was once again blemished by a deep rectangular hole. It was as though this very spot, just like my life, was ruptured again, the once-familiar and continuous now open and raw.

Beside the hole was a pile of dirt covered with a green cloth. Some folding wooden chairs had been set up nearby by someone who knew that mourners need a place to sit. In them were my parents' friends, old people whose heads all turned toward me as I approached. I was, after all, the male child, expected to say the memorial prayers when a parent dies in traditional Jewish society.

My family, however, had never observed the religion of our ancestors, so I knew no prayers. And there were no parents there to take charge, so I just stood there, awkwardly staring back, my eyes burning from held-back tears, as my parents' friends sat staring at me. I closed my eyes.

I felt six years old. I remembered being six. A supermarket had just opened in our neighborhood. Until then, we had had to go many blocks to a farmer's market for our meat and produce. Shopping was a daily activity. But now, my parents had said, we could get fresh food right in the neighborhood.

I remember two important events from my young life involving that store. The first was my introduction to the automatically opening grocery store door that opened as you passed through a beam of light. It was like magic. "Swish" it opened. "Swish" it closed. Nothing to do but keep walking. I remember standing there, in astonishment, as my normally dignified and shy father circled in and out of the store, his long wool coat flapping behind his slightly stooped back. In the "in" door and out the "out" door, he strode, the swishing and clattering doors punctuating his breathless demonstration of this latest development by "dece ah-mace-ink Ah-mer-ee-kance." I had never witnessed such animation from my father. That day we walked home holding hands.

The other event, the one I was probably reminded of in the cemetery, was when, wandering among the aisles and studying the colorful merchandise on the shelves and the debris on the floor with equal interest, I suddenly realized that my mother and I were no longer together. My body went cold, my breathing stopped, and my eyes burned. I remembered that panic so clearly, when I ran up and down the aisles screaming, "Mommy. Mommy. Mommy." I remembered seeing a pair of lady's legs and a skirt. Sobbing, I ran right into them and dove for safety.

Wrong lady. Struggling to keep her balance, she asked, "What's the matter, honey, have you lost your mommy?"

Just then, my worried-looking mother came around the end of the aisle and reclaimed me, roughly pulling me back to our grocery cart.

It did not matter that I felt six years old in the cemetery. I knew there would be no tearful reunion this time. No scolding, huge-hugging, treat-buying, hand-holding conclusion to the adventure. No return to the familiar. No smiling materialization. No embrace. No funny story at dinner.

And there sat those old people beside my parents' grave. If any of them had asked me that same question, "What's the matter, honey, have you lost your mommy?" I could have begun sobbing then, too.

There is no experience quite as stunning as when there is nothing where something has always been. To try and imagine the absence of something is to imagine the thing itself, not the hole left behind. Especially when that thing has the first face you probably ever saw, spoke the first words you ever heard, and whose touch has comforted and guided and corrected and made you safe since the beginning of time.

Parents just are. They are a constant in the lives of their children. From an infant's first gasping breaths, parents, or some other adult parental figures with whom the infant can bond, must consistently and effectively provide or the infant does not survive. Oxygen, liquids, food, rest, protection from predators and extremes of temperature—these are the basics without which children will not long exist. They are a continuous necessity; monitoring them requires constant vigilance. The image of the timeless parent is inseparable from the essentials that they furnish.

I began investigating the subject of adult parental bereavement. I read most of what's been written on the subject in the popular, medical, and psychological literature surprisingly quickly—a comment on the dearth of material rather than on my reading speed.

I found the material quite interesting, but what was even more interesting was how little material there was. This was a surprise because, after all, parental death is the single most common cause of bereavement in this country. Nearly 12 million adults, or 5 percent of the population, lose a parent each year. Numerically, parental death has the highest incidence in the "death of a family member" category. Parental loss is not the province of an unfortunate few. It is the ultimate equal-opportunity experience, requiring nothing other than children not predeceasing their parents.

Nonetheless, the term "death of a family member," at least as it is used in the psychological and medical literature, is most likely to refer to the death of a spouse. It is next most likely to refer to the death of a child. It is significantly less likely to refer to death of a parent, and it virtually never refers to death of a sibling.

When someone writes about the effects of parental death on adults, they typically focus on the ramifications of the loss of parent(s) during childhood. There are studies, reports, and essays on the dreams of the dying, the mental status of those who provide care to the dying, the various ways people die, the various choices people can and should be able to make regarding their own dying, and even bereavement following the loss of a pet (people in this last category have their own group support network).

These subjects, like all other aspects of the human condition, are interesting, important, and worthy of investigation. But I do keep wondering why becoming an orphan as an adult receives so little attention.

As a psychologist, I have witnessed many people becoming orphans as adults, and they always describe significant life change associated with that loss. The accompanying feelings most often are described as being "surprisingly intense," a phrase that implies, "I know this isn't a big deal for most people, but it sure is a big deal to me."

Parental loss is inevitable, and everyone seems to agree that it is a crisis. So why is it not talked about much, not written about much, not studied much?

"There appears to be impatience with the grief of a bereaved adult child," writes Catherine Sanders in *Grief: The Mourning After*, a 1989 examination of types of loss. "People rarely inquire into the personal feelings of these bereaved or acknowledge their grief after a week or two, as though it does not require much attention or long-term reaction. Adult orphaned children must keep their feelings to themselves and mourn in secret."

Sanders further suggests that little attention is devoted to the study of the effect of the death of parents on surviving adult children because this is regarded as part of the "natural order of universal dynamics." Why, however, this would be considered more a part of the natural order than any other more widely researched or discussed subject of less frequency, like the loss of a spouse or a child, is a mystery to me.

Can it be, wonder Miriam and Sidney Moss, among the very few researchers with more than one publication on this topic, that we value youth so much that the lives and deaths of older people decrease in social value? If so, perhaps the expression of grief at the loss of a very old person is considered less socially meaningful, with the expectation being that the mourner needs less comfort.

Or might it be, I sometimes wonder, that the growing value our society puts on the rights and privileges of individuals has progressed to such an extent that we have become preoccupied with ourselves, our own rights, and our own comforts at the expense of any compassionate involvement with one another?

Such intense focus on ourselves leaves little room in our hearts for experience other than our own, let alone the disruptive and confusing emotions of others. The suffering of others—to which we cannot relate and from which we therefore believe we will be spared—begins to bear no relevance for us. We are unmoved by it. It is an annoyance and a bother. We just want the sufferer to "get over it."

We in Western culture currently consider death formidable and avoidable. We avoid thinking about it. We avoid preparing for it. We almost never talk about it, and when we do, we avoid saying its name.

A few years ago, I asked one of my daughter's friends from childhood if she wanted to go with us to the funeral of someone we all knew. She replied, "No, that's all right. Thanks anyway, but I don't do that death thing."

It sounded funny. So charmingly naive. But the more I think about it, the more I think that most of us don't do "that death thing."

People have told me that they even consider death an insult, the ultimate humiliation, a contradiction to life. Physicians, who on a daily basis deal with issues of life and death, have told me that they don't like to admit that the best they can do is relieve discomfort and postpone death. Rather, they prefer to call what they do "saving lives."

We avoid looking at death directly, as if trying to avoid eye contact with the playground bully, in the belief that if he doesn't notice us, he'll leave us alone. And yet the more we try to avoid facing the bully, the more menacing he becomes.

I believe our attitude toward death is a fairly recent development in the history of Western culture. As recently as the beginning of this century, death was considered a feature of ordinary life. Families were large, usually tightly knit. Everyone lived close by. Someone was always being born, and someone was always dying. Both happened at home. There was hardly a year during which some close relative did not succumb. Corpses of the young and the old alike were prepared for burial by the family, laid out in the parlor, and collectively mourned.

But we in contemporary Western culture try to have as little to do with death as we can. We exclude the dying from family life; they are dispatched to the hospital. We no longer wash and dress the dead, nor do we surrender our homes to their remains; all that is handled now by the funeral industry. We no longer even suspend our routines to grieve—a few days off and then it's back to work. Death has been sanitized and institutionalized.

Our economic and political philosophies stress the individual. We cherish ourselves and each other. We celebrate living. We treasure opportunities. We hold that people have rights, paramount among which are the rights to life, liberty, and the pursuit of happiness, unfettered by distinctions of class, race, gender, religion, or national origin as in the past. We reject such limits. We reject all limits.

We celebrate life, and we leave death out of the party.

We grow up being told, "You can become anything you want to be." We are never told, "Actually, there is an end to your pursuit, no matter how accomplished or grand or fulfilled you become. Its name is death." Our image of life, and of ourselves, does not embrace this, the ultimate in equal opportunity.

Traditional limits just no longer apply. The food we all eat is now produced by a tiny fraction of our population. Ordinary people own and control huge tracts of land, factories, or other means of production. Actual work is done by machines. Modern methods of storing and transporting have made accumulation possible—the more, the better. All of this was inconceivable a century ago. Virtually boundless wealth can be amassed. What once would have been called greed is now considered a sign of success.

We grow up being told, "The sky's the limit." We are never told, "Actually, there is an outer boundary to your attainment, no matter how much you manage to accumulate, and its name is death."

No longer are we at the mercy of people in specialized positions of authority with esoteric access to secret knowledge. Someone with nominal research skills can now learn as much as a doctor knows about a particular medical condition, including alternative treatment methods and the side effects of specific medications.

Illumination is available to everyone, but we have little curiosity about the contents of life's shadows. We grow up being told, "Your knowledge is limited only by your imagination." We are never told, "Actually, there is an outer boundary to what can be known, a dimension of the truth that shall forever evade understanding, and its name is death."

Travel used to be limited to the physical endurance of a person or the animal on which the person rode. Now, any of us could replicate Marco Polo's journey and be home in time for supper on the supersonic overnight flight. What was formerly unthinkable has become routine, and the formerly amazing has become ordinary.

Time and space are now malleable ideas rather than absolute limits of reality. If we miss seeing the big play of the game, it'll be shown on the instant replay. If we wish we'd seen it from another angle, they'll show that, too. If we're too busy to go see a movie, it'll be on television. If we're too busy to watch the broadcast, we can just program the VCR. Death. Finality. Such unfashionable notions are just too confining for us and our advanced ways.

But inevitably, death comes and takes a loved one. Shocking! A blow to our understanding of our big and powerful masters-of-the-universe selves. And when death first comes, typically, it takes one of our parents.

It is a cultural fiction that parental death is an incidental experience of adult life. If one of the purposes of culture is to provide us with a map—navigational assistance as we move into each stage of life—then this particular bit of misinformation beguiles us. Imagine a map that failed to correctly show a huge turn in the road, beyond which lay a dramatically different terrain in which many road signs change meaning. Perhaps this cultural falsehood supports and promotes certain social and material values, but it does not serve us well since it so poorly equips us for the actual experience when it occurs.

The maps of antiquity were drawn with borders of dragons and serpents to differentiate the known terrain, with its explored forests and rivers, from the vast and yet unexplored territories beyond, filled with the fearsome dangers that always seem to lurk in the unknown. Our culture does not supply a map with a border of dragons to warn us that things will be different beyond a certain point. As a result, each of us is caught by surprise when we move beyond the limit of our parents' lives.

My daughter's college boyfriend told me that as a child, he had assumed most grown-ups got over the death of their parents within two weeks. He had concluded this, reasonably enough, from his observations in high school that teachers whose parents died generally took a leave of absence for about two weeks and then returned to work appearing none the worse for wear. He had always worried, he said, because he believed it was going to be a bigger deal for him than that.

Within months of my mother's death, it appeared I had gotten my life pretty much back "on course." The financial matters had been turned over to lawyers, my parents' distant friends had been notified, the "stuff" had been distributed, and both my sister and I were doing fine. About eight months later, however, my mood suddenly began to deteriorate. Ordinarily optimistic and cheerful, I became sullen and withdrawn. I lost weight, developed difficulty concentrating, and became easily confused. Strange and somewhat troubling, this gradual unraveling was best defined by its vagueness. It didn't appear to be "about" anything. Although I could characterize the mood with words like "vexed," "woeful," "melancholy," and "despondent," I could neither attribute it to a cause nor organize it around any issues.

I made an appointment with my doctor when this odd feeling persisted into its fourth week. I was concerned that having such a strange and unfocused feeling descend on me for no apparent reason and with no particular form might indicate a disease. Might I have a brain tumor? Was I developing diabetes? Was I going crazy?

As I stood downstairs in the medical office building waiting for an elevator, I stared out through the glass doors into the street. It was a bright and sunny day and the colorfully dressed pedestrians provided a diversion as they passed by the huge glass doors that lined the front of the building. The "ding" of the arriving elevator to my left only slightly drew my attention to the periphery of my visual field as I heard the elevator door open. I gasped before even registering what I saw.

I recognized the feeling, immediately. I remembered it from when I was a child, from the time when I couldn't find my mother in the new neighborhood grocery store with the automatic doors. I remembered it from when I carried her cremated remains to the grave on the day of her burial.

As I watched the three very tiny old ladies shuffle out of the elevator, pass me in the lobby, and go out into the sunshine, I had tears in my eyes for the first time since my mother died.

In the doctor's office, I began describing the strange mood shifts and other changes of the past months, while in the back of my mind I pondered what had just happened. The doctor asked, "What do you suppose has been going on?"

I unhesitatingly answered, "Nothing. Nothing is going on. Particularly the 'nothing' that remains now that both of my parents are dead. And this 'nothing' keeps on going on."

Only then was I able to begin facing and actively grieving over the losses of my parents and all the precious protective illusions that had died with them.

In these past years, I have been asking and learning quite a lot about what happens when adults become orphans. For the most part, I have learned that the relationship between children and their parents, regardless of its quality or content, is unbreakable by death. Parents play an entirely unique role: Whatever else can be said about them, they are the first and the most prominent continuous certainty in our lives. We are aware of them before we become aware of anything else. We have gotten used to them before we even learn of life's other constants like the sun, the moon, or the ground.

Whatever our relationship with them and however well or poorly we get along, parents project an illusion of permanence, a constancy that suggests life to be a knowable, reliable, trustworthy, and, therefore, feasible endeavor.

It's not that we see parents as impregnable. Throughout our lives, we see them beset by all kinds of life hazards. We watch them get sick—a cold in summer, the flu in winter, headache, sore throat, infection. They may get injured. They feel lousy. For a while. And then we watch them get better. They may not always get completely better. They might limp or have a scar, but for the most part, we see them go beyond injury and persevere, and our belief in parental durability is buttressed every time.

Their infirmities may be disruptive to regular family life; they may be inconvenient; they may even be frightening. But, throughout our lives, we see parental sickness as transient. Parents, on the other hand, are enduring.

But ultimately, the phone rings or a letter arrives or we visit the hospital, and we are told that our parents, sick or injured, won't bounce back. We may watch them linger, impaired for a while, before they start to decline, or they may go quickly, even unexpectedly. How ever it happens, without exception, parents die.

And as we watch them vanish, slipping beyond our grasp, we feel a part of that innocent sense of safety and security, unwittingly based on a lifetime's exposure to the appearance of parental permanence, vanishing as well.

The playground bully finally gets us.

And then a lot may begin to change. At a minimum, parental death in midlife elicits lingering feelings of loneliness, memories of former losses, unresolved conflicts, and doubts concerning life's purpose.

Interpersonal relationships may be affected. There is frequently upheaval in a love relationship within months of one of the partners' losing a parent. Family roles among siblings may be reassigned as patterns of intimacy, caring, commitment, family identity, and support are reorganized. Old friendships sometimes wither. New friendships may form.

How we think and spend time may change. For instance, by 1900, Mary Kingsley had explored and chronicled hundreds of miles of the wild Ogowe and Rembwe Rivers in West Africa, places no European had ever been. She began this unusual occupation shortly after both her parents died. Likewise, Sigmund Freud announced the "discovery" of the Oedipus complex, a theory about the male child's struggle with the image of his father, one year after the death of his own father.

There is a sudden awareness of no longer being someone's child, which carries with it a loss of childhood altogether. Feeling "adult," a member of the eldest generation, brings the chilling knowledge that there is now no one between us and death.

Without exception, those with whom I have spoken soon after the death of their second parent have said to me, "I just realized that I am the next in line to die."

There may even be changes in health and mental health associated with parental loss. There is research that suggests that the death of a parent is a significant precursor to mental disorder for both men and women. There is, in fact, a significant increase in suicide rates within a month of the anniversary of parental death. Mortality rates, in general, among recently bereaved relatives is seven times greater than normal within six months of the death.

Mourning is not just the process of getting over a loss and getting on with one's life. It is a transition. And change is the hallmark of transition.

Although the process of mourning may gradually approach resolution, the grief is never over. Memories and feelings associated with parents occur many times throughout the years following their deaths. For some, these may be welcome visits from the beloved departed. For others, or at other times, they may, instead, seem like painful and frightening hauntings.

Sometimes memories occur when the survivor least expects them. While walking to my office recently, I overtook a sixtyish woman who works in the same building as I do. We know each other only casually from seeing one another and exchanging pleasantries in the elevators and coffee shop through the years. I know her name. She knows mine.

It was a pleasant spring day and we walked together, making small talk. Invariably cheerful and outgoing, she innocently inquired about the large package I was carrying. Since it contained materials for this book, I answered by mentioning the subject of losing parents as adults. I heard her sucking in breath. She grew quiet and slowed her stride. Finally, clearing her throat and wiping her eyes, she began to speak about the loss of her father, twenty years previously, and the enormous impact his, and her mother's, death had had on her. I responded with a brief description of my own losses and their effects on me. We walked those last few blocks more slowly, each holding on to and comforted by the unanticipated discovery of our shared experience.

Since that day, I am aware that those I pass while walking to my office may also have already crossed the threshold of parental loss. How helpful it would be, I think, if we knew about each other and the common features of our experiences. How might it be for the others, those still inside the margins of the conventional map, if they knew what awaits them and what constitutes the boundary.

What would it be helpful for them to know? Can they be informed that becoming an orphan is part of being an adult, that it is likely to happen to all of us, that many others have gone there, and that the journey into this alien experience is already somewhat charted? Might those of us already traversing the dragon-filled territory beyond the border of life's map reassure those still in the familiar terrain of living parents that pathways through the unexplored abound and that the land of serpents is not dangerous, however frightful it may appear?

So, twice a year, once in the spring and once in the fall, after I travel to a cemetery on the other side of town, I sit against a warm headstone and, looking out where so many others have buried their parents, wonder about many things, especially about how strange an experience it is to have become an orphan as an adult.

Remembering My Father

We're sitting on the porch swing
and it's way after dark,
the summer night is a soft blanket, so
tell me again about going on the train.

Let's pretend
Mama hasn't died yet
I never grew up and went away
(making you laugh and cry
packing jeans for my honeymoon)
and never bore a baby boy
or offered to carry your visiting suitcase
at the station.
You said Wait till I'm eighty,
then you can.

O Daddy, you never got to eighty,
never did let your youngest
carry the suitcase
when you went on the train.

Tell me again in the quiet now
(the only sounds are the swing chains creaking
and june bugs pinging on the screen)
how to say moon in Spanish

and please once more
about going on the train.

—Roberta Goodwin
Los Angeles, CA

GOOD GRIEF!

Aspects of Grief Associated with Parental Death

What good is grief? People are supposed to die. Why do we suffer so terribly when they do?

Especially when old parents die, why should that be so difficult? After all, everyone must die sometime, and old parents are, well, old. They have already lived a long time, and their lives are generally as full as they are going to get. They are often sick. They are often living lives of diminished quality and few pleasures. It is time for them to join the dead. And yet, when they die, we grieve.

When we sprain an ankle, it hurts. This pain lets us know that something is wrong. It forces us to keep our weight off the injury so as to not cause further harm. This pain serves a purpose. Grief hurts, too, but does it serve a purpose? Is it trying to let us know something? I believe the answer is yes.

But first, it would help to define grief. What is it? Everybody experiences it, but how can we define it?

Some thinkers have said that grief is instinctive, a reaction to a disruption in the constancy of our self-image. They believe grief to be a trauma to the primitive core of our personality, precipitated by the loss of a loved one.

Others have proposed that grief is interpersonal rather than intrapersonal. They believe grief is a reaction to the disruption in the way we relate to the people and world around us because someone we love has died.

Others suggest grief is culturally determined, having little to do with the individual. Rather, they believe grief is a learned phenomenon, like preferences in music and reactions to art, created and shaped by social norms and expectations.

Another group with a theory, the Poso natives of Central Madagascar, believe that grief is a natural tribute to the Original Couple and their sacrifices during the time of Creation. According to legend, the Creator offered the Posos' original ancestors a stone and a banana as gifts. Hungry, they chose the banana and ignored the stone. The Creator then announced that because they had chosen the banana rather than the stone, their lives, and the lives of their descendants, would be patterned after that of the banana.

Since the banana's parent stem dies after producing fruit, humans, too, would produce offspring and then die. Had the Original Couple accepted the gift of the stone, human life would have been patterned after the stone—barren and immortal.

When Poso natives grieve, they are not remembering the individual member of their community who has died. Instead, they are commemorating the altruism of their original ancestors, and all subsequent generations, who made life possible for them.

In some academic psychological circles, attention has shifted away from defining what grief is. The thinkers of this culture are instead becoming more interested in the component properties of grief, that is, what constitutes grief itself. Much of what they believe about how we grieve was adapted from Elisabeth Kubler-Ross's pioneering work in the 1960s and 1970s on the experiences of the dying, the theory being that coming to grips with one's own dying is similar to coming to grips with the dying of any loved one. I can understand how conceptualizing grief as a phenomenon in such organized and systematic ways is helpful for instructional purposes in college classrooms. I can also understand how such an orderly introduction to some of grief's dimensions could be reassuring to the bereft, who may be somewhat surprised and horrified by the unattractive and unsympathetic feelings they are encountering. But I don't think this methodical model, despite its inclusion here, has very much to do with the actual experience of grief.

For what they're worth, these are the conventional stages of grief:

Disbelief, avoidance, and denial. In grief's earliest stages, there is a period of vacillation between icy fear and numbness, during which we attempt to retreat from the conflict of, on the one hand, knowing that someone we love has died, while, on the other hand, not being able to believe that they are gone. We may walk around confused or we may distract ourselves by getting busy, making arrangements for the disposal of parents' things, seeing to legal matters, getting extra busy at work—doing anything we can to get our minds off the losses we know we have suffered and cannot comprehend.

Anger. Next, energy begins to form and gets directed at the deceased (for not taking better care of themselves), at medical people (for not having done more), at family members and friends (for countless real or imagined shortcomings), and at God (for allowing such suffering). Anger also gets deflected into combative attitudes and behavior toward people who have nothing, whatever, to do with the loss. This protest is one of our ways of struggling to comprehend the incomprehensible. We feel a need to make sense of things, even things of which sense cannot be made. We believe we will feel better if we can find a cause, and therefore someone or something to blame, for our loss.

Guilt. Next, the anger is said to get turned back on ourselves. Our mistakes, omissions, and shortcomings toward the deceased, throughout their lives as well as during their final illness, are mercilessly and redundantly examined. We may blame ourselves for their death or their suffering or the lack of attention we paid them. Nothing we have done or omitted escapes our critical review, no blunder is overlooked, no lapse feels forgivable.

Surrender to sorrow. Next, when the protection of denial, anger, avoidance, and guilt have faded, the reality of our loss washes over us. It is a time of fear and sadness, when we feel empty, despairing, and lost. We acutely miss the deceased, and we long for their release from death. We might cry, or at the least, we might wish we could.

Acceptance. Eventually we arrive at a peaceful acknowledgment that our loss is permanent, and the absence of the deceased becomes an integrated fact in our permanent worldview. We no longer acutely and continuously miss or think about those we have lost. We remember and miss them, to be sure, but when we do, it is without the unbearably wrenching distress we felt when grief was new.

In addition to such a paradigm being something of a misrepresentation of what goes on when we grieve, there's a drawback to creating false expectations of orderly grieving among the newly bereft. This pitfall was brought into focus for me, years ago, when an impeccably dressed, matronly woman came to see me for a consultation. She described, in great detail, the steps she had been taking to redirect her life since her mother's death, four years previously. She had dedicated most of her adult life to caring for her mother, especially during the last years of her mother's life, and the old woman's death had left a huge hole that she had been, to date unsuccessfully, trying to fill. She had tried joining various clubs, had taken tours to places she had always wanted to visit, and had even enrolled in an adult education course in Italian cooking. When she concluded that none of these steps were producing the desired results of setting her free from the distress of her loss, she decided to seek professional help.

During our initial conversation, I asked how she had mourned after her mother died and what her grief had been like. "Oh," she said, "that wasn't so easy. I read a book about it, and really tried to get into it. But every time I would begin, I'd just start to cry, and I'd have to start all over again."

During our many subsequent meetings, she reminisced about her long and complicated relationship with her mother. She cried a lot. She laughed. She trembled. She raged. There was no order to her emotional states, nor, she found, did she need it. For one entire session, she sat with a package of family photographs, which she had brought to show me, unopened in her lap while she sobbed. In another session, she told me hilarious stories about her mother's parsimonious methods of cutting financial corners. I did not name any of her emotions, nor did I identify any "stages" as she shared her stories with me. Rather, I received and welcomed whatever arrived. I trusted that when she was remembering, sharing, wailing, raging, laughing, or crying, she was grieving.

Within a few months of coming to see me, she was finding some peace regarding her mother's life and death. By the end of that year, she had become more able to claim herself as an individual, independent of her mother, and she was ready to move into a future lacking the illusions of certainty and reliability her mother had always represented for her. At the end of our final appointment, she left to meet with a realtor, finally able to have her mother's house put up for sale. The next day she called to tell me that she was feeling sad and free, both at the same time, and to get one final reassurance that those are the tangled and complicated dimensions of grief.

I have found that whenever people recount stories of their grief to me, no one ever speaks about a sequential, organized experience. They talk about a hodgepodge of moments, given texture and meaning by emotions like fear, pain, shame, and joy, and they call this jumble "grief."

They speak about such terrible fears as the fear that they will never feel better or the fear that they will never stop crying or the fear that something is wrong with them because they really do not feel all that upset and have not yet begun to cry. They talk about persistent and insatiable wishes that they had said "I love you," just once more, before the end. They talk about their confusion over other people's impatience with their sadness. They tell me how surprised they are by how much they miss the deceased. More shamefully, but just as frequently, they talk about how surprised they are by how little they miss the deceased. They timidly confess the joy they are finding in newfound freedoms. They describe night terrors in which they abruptly awaken and find themselves drenched in sweat, standing beside their bed, screaming at a rapidly dissolving vision from a fading dream. They speak with embarrassment about the unattractive qualities they are discovering in themselves like pettiness, greed, or moodiness. They talk about how weird everything now seems, even though only a little bit has changed.

Sometimes they can't talk to me at all. Instead, they can only sob the heartbroken sob of the inconsolable infant or scream the frightened scream of the newborn or rage the purple breath-holding fury of the frustrated toddler.

Pretending that grief—which really is a fundamental and primitive experience—takes place in our minds or that it can be conceptually organized and "understood" is to risk misrepresenting grief's chaotic power and to risk missing grief's point altogether.

So, what is grief? And why do we grieve?

I think grief is an expression of our fundamental inability to comprehend, conceptually or any other way, that a loved one has died. Our brains don't work that way. We can't help it.

We are accustomed to a person coming back into the room after that person has left it. We cannot form an affirmative mental image of someone who has always been there no longer being anywhere. We simply cannot imagine someone whom we once knew alive being not alive.

We cannot conceive of ourselves being without someone who is precious to us, and yet when someone important to us dies, even though we can't conceive it has happened, we strain to grasp their absence. That's the way our brain works. We can't help it.

And so, leaning forward to reach out and embrace the familiar image of someone who is no longer there, we fall into the abyss their absence has left behind. We tumble into endless emptiness, and we are enveloped by the dark and suffocating uncertainty of life's most confounding and distressing dilemmas: that despite comforting illusions of vigor and youthfulness, our lives are fragile, and we are attached to them by no more than the slender thread of fortune's whimsy; that regardless of how self-sufficient, successful, and clever we may be, we are profoundly dependent on those we love; that no veneer of professional expertise, adult accomplishment, or social self-confidence can effectively camouflage our underlying and awesome terror of the unknown; and that no matter how much we know or how strong our faith, we stand powerless and helpless in the face of life's impenetrable mysteries.

This plunge into, and temporary consumption by, life's fragility and mystery *is*, in my opinion, grief. A time of distress and disorientation, it also has the capacity to be one of life's most liberating and transforming opportunities.

Sometimes bereft people who feel stuck in grief come to me for help. They say, in essence: "I think something's wrong. Someone I love died, and I have been upset about it for a long time. I know they're dead, and I should be feeling bad for them, but I'm just feeling bad. I've got to stop being so upset. It's not doing me any good. I'm not the only one who thinks so. Everyone says that it's time for me to get over it, get back to my real life, and put all this behind me. But even though I agree I should be done with it, I can't seem to get over it. What's wrong with me?"

My response is: Welcome to the world of the bereft. This is not a diversion from your real life. This is not an exercise made up of a set of stages—one, two, three, four, five—that you have to go through before getting back to your real life. This *is* your real life. You really have sustained that loss. You really are going to live the rest of your life without that precious person. Neither I nor anyone else can help you put that behind you. No one can help you to get "over it." You don't need to. Grief is something you get through, and if you let it get through you as well, you will eventually find that you have enough room in yourself to contain it. And when you come out the other side of this terrible time, without needing to understand how it happened any more than you need to understand how you digest food and distribute nutrients throughout your body in order to be well fed, you will find that you are able to face, and conduct, your life in a new way.

People rarely understand these words when I say them. Most of us are not accustomed to thinking about grief at all, so the idea that there is a "world of the bereft" seems strange—to say nothing of being welcomed to it. It's not even always so easy to know when we are there.

Grief is not always easy to recognize. Like a fingerprint, each person's grief is unique. There are no standards for grief, no natural history. Some may experience acute grief for only twenty minutes, and it may make their head feel on fire. Others' grief may last for twenty years as a persistent dull ache. One person may be briefly and vaguely distracted by grief. Others may have long periods of intense preoccupation with their sorrow, times during which all other mental activity ceases. One person may be composed while grieving and feel anguish. Another may flail and howl and feel numb. For one person, the prevailing emotion that emerges may be sadness, for another it may be anger, and for yet another it may be blessed relief.

Grief often arrives disguised. I have known people to temporarily lose interest in sex and believe the problem was in their marriage but later realize that it was grief. I have known people to start craving afternoon naps, and it was grief. Some people are fine for years after a loss, and then, with no apparent provocation, they collapse into profound depression, and that, too, is grief. A sudden interest in work, lost interest in food, an intense need to shop or even shoplift, changes of any type—all these may be masked grief. Some people remain calm while grieving; others have unexpected, rapid, and seemingly unprovoked shifts in mood. For some, emotional states may appear and disappear, fade in and out of one another, weave around each other, tangling, contaminating, and compounding, with neither apparent transitions nor evident purpose.

Grief is often characterized by disorientation. We become temporarily lost when a familiar and important part of our world has disappeared. We may have trouble differentiating the familiar from the unfamiliar at such times. I remember walking into the hospital emergency parking area on the day my mother died, amazed by the vividness and richness of the colors around me yet unable to figure out which car in the lot was mine.

I have heard people refer to grief as a type of mutilation: "I feel like I've lost a part of myself," "I feel like part of me is missing," "It's like part of my heart is gone." Jason, a fifty-eight-year-old married onetime battlefield medic, told me that this sense of being maimed reminded him of a phenomenon called "phantom limb" among amputees, in which they still experienced itching and other sensations in the missing limb.

Jason told me that after his parents died, he would still start to call them to share an anecdote, only to remember that their number had been disconnected. Like the amputees, he said, he often reaches to scratch what's missing and is surprised, each time, to discover nothing there.

Not everyone will lose a spouse, siblings, or children, but all of us are guaranteed to experience parental grief if only we live long enough. For this and many other reasons, parental grief is unique from grief in general. This is not surprising since the relationship we have with parents is unlike any other relationship we have in our lives.

However, because we have two parents, we have two different experiences with parental death and grief. Even in the exceedingly rare event of both parents perishing at the same time because of the same catastrophe—say, an automobile accident or a house fire—our experience is still different for each because of gender, order, and specifics of death and the nature of the relationship we had with each of them. In the more typical circumstance of parents dying sequentially, our experience of each is different for all the reasons above, in addition to the difference between the first and second deaths.

Parents provide a unique spot on this planet, which is called "home," where we can return, if we need to, to be loved and to feel that we belong. This spot, in the parent's heart and in our mind, has existed from the beginning of our lives, and it has flourished in shared ancestry with roots stretching back to the beginning of time. It exists whether parents are kind or unkind, attentive or neglectful, young or old, healthy or sick, living in the family home or in a nursing facility. This spot cannot be imitated. It cannot be recreated. There is only one spot that is ever the real spot called home.

After parents die, it's gone. The unfathomable loss of that "spot called home," regardless of its location or the quality of what actually occurred there when parents were living, is a recurrent theme in many parental bereavement stories.

If parents were supportive and encouraging, these deaths mark the end of access to such reassurance. I still remember the sobs of a client, over fifteen years ago, as she wailed when her beloved mother died, "No one will ever love me like that again. No one will ever again think that whatever I do is great. No one will ever be proud of me or brag about me or always take my side no matter what I've done."

This is not the universal cry, however, of the parentally bereft. Of course, those with relationships they enjoyed grieve what is lost. Those with relationships they despised, by contrast, grieve the loss of hope for change.

Sometimes even those who have a parent who left in their infancy and who have no memory of that parent whatsoever are surprised by a profound sense of loss if they learn of that missing parent's death. And they may be further surprised to learn that they had fostered lifelong fantasies of reconciliation, substitutes for that spot called home, which suddenly became impossible because it could no longer be realized.

Inconceivable though it may be, even those who have murdered a mother or father in a desperate act of self-protection in the face of intolerable abuse may be dismayed to find that they experience a deep sense of loss afterward when they realize that the voluntary change they longed for from that parent has been precluded.

Most of us had complex relationships with our parents, which we sometimes enjoyed and sometimes loathed, which were sometimes gentle and sometimes harsh. When our parents die, those details no longer matter. Our spot called "home" is gone, and we grieve its heretofore unimaginable loss.

The time in adult life prior to the first parent's death is not a time of ignorance: It's not as though we don't all know that someday our parents will die, that we will grieve, that then we will live the rest of our lives without them. Rather, it is a time of innocence: Knowing that parents will die does not carry within its wisdom any hint of the impact the experience will have. I suppose Dorothy could have predicted that things would be different after a tornado, but finding herself in Oz when the wind died down must have been quite a surprise.

Some people have mentioned to me that it feels like they begin an entirely new life when their first parent dies. And in many ways, they do. No matter the diligence devoted to maintaining familiar and accustomed patterns of life and traditional family activities after this first death, everything has already begun to change. For instance, even if a holiday is celebrated in exactly the same location and in exactly the same way as it always was, it feels different than it once did because everyone sitting at the table is acutely aware of the missing parent's absence. This is not limited to Norman Rockwellesque family holiday gatherings. I remember being told by a friend, years after the death of his insufferable father, a man who made every family get-together a fiasco with his loud and inconsiderate conduct, "The holidays just aren't the same since Dad died."

So many details of life change after the first parent dies—and our grief is made manifest with each jolting awareness. Calling home becomes subtly different because of who doesn't answer. Buying presents for the holidays becomes different because of the presents we see that remind us that we have a shorter list than we used to. Nearly everything becomes somewhat different than it used to be.

A hallmark of the period after the first parent dies is a change in the relationship with the remaining parent. Grief can get somewhat diffused—or perhaps more accurately, it can be postponed—by the requirements of this new relationship. If parents are married and living together at the time the first one dies, grief is usually considered the domain of the surviving parent. Their needs and grief take precedence. The role of surviving adult children is typically to aid the bereaved widow or widower rather than to be the primary mourner. There may be financial or domestic arrangements to be made for the surviving parent, along with countless problems to be solved. The typical inquiry by others is "How's your mom/dad (surviving parent) doing?" rather than "How are you doing?"

As surviving parents rebuild a life that no longer includes their spouse, they may become increasingly unrecognizable and alien to their children. Holidays really feel different the first time Dad or Mom brings his or her new love interest to dinner.

If parents were divorced or separated, as is increasingly the case, and if the kids maintained a relationship with both parents, the death of the first parent can mark an end to the loyalty conflict and complicated visitation patterns that often distinguish such arrangements. These children are now free to form and develop a new and unopposed relationship with the remaining parent or step-parent.

When the first parent dies, we begin a distinctive period of adulthood that continues until the death of the second parent. This first death sets up an expectant state, similar to that of awaiting the crash after hearing the screeching tires that herald an imminent collision. This vague anxiety, which can become a low-grade depression if it lasts a long time, generally persists for the duration of the surviving parent's life.

When the second parent dies, the rest of adulthood begins. To some degree, the impact of this second loss is a function of the duration between parents' deaths and, much more so, of the nature of their deaths. No parental death is uncomplicated, but some are more complicated than others. Some parents die quietly and gracefully, smiling fondly at loved ones gathered bedside, who are, tearfully, smiling back as they slip away. Others linger in coma for weeks and months, draining family resources, patience, and goodwill. Others spend their final days screaming in pain and frustration, hurling hateful invectives at their horrified and heartbroken families, and cursing the impotence of the medical profession for its failure to provide relief. Some die after prolonged illnesses during which they and their adult children have time to speak about shared times and shared memories. Some die suddenly, in the unexpected grip of some massive medical crisis. Some die violently in fiery automobile accidents or other disasters. Some—in fact, a growing number in current years—commit suicide.

In such an extreme instance, as when the parent has committed suicide—or in the even more extreme instance when the parent has enlisted an adult child to assist in their suicide, either because of incapacity brought on by the ravages of some debilitating disease or because of a failure in suicidal resolve on their part—recovery from the acute portion of the grief will take much longer and be much more painful than if the parent dies from a brief but terminal illness during which their outlook remained cheerful and upbeat. The addition of shock, horror, bewilderment, and disbelief to the ordinary mixture of emotion that accompanies loss compounds and intensifies the experience Emily Dickinson called "the hour of lead."

We do not get to select when or how our parents die, but as a rule, the more anticipatable and the less violent or grotesque the deaths, the simpler the grief of the survivors. Long periods of illness and steady declines raise different issues than sudden or violent deaths.

There are certain feelings that typically linger after parents die. For instance, I feel lingering regret since the deaths of each of my parents, although what I regret is different with each of them. My father died unexpectedly, after serious surgery from which he never fully regained consciousness. It had not occurred to me that he was in danger of dying when he entered the hospital, despite his advanced age. It was quite a shock hearing the doctor say that my father would not emerge from the coma. I do not think that the unreality of his death would have been much different, though, even had I been more able to anticipate it.

My recurrent regret, since his death, has been that I did not know he would die so quickly. There were so many conversations I wish I had tried to have with him, so many questions I would have liked to have asked. I wish I had asked him to describe for me the inside of his parents' home or tell me about the games he played with his brothers and sister as a youngster. I doubt that those conversations, had they occurred, would have been particularly satisfying. My father had been somewhat severe and unforthcoming with me throughout my life, and I doubt he would have suddenly become more open to me at the end. But I wish I had known to try one more time. Not having taken that one last pass at knowing him better leaves me wondering.

My mother's death was completely different. She succumbed after a very long battle with the ravages of old age, complete with its most unattractive mental and physical decay. Becoming increasingly demented and frail with each passing month, she seemed to meander toward death, taking brutal and tedious years to stroll what seemed, at the time, the short distance from dementia to grave. She was repeatedly pulled back from death's clasp by antibiotics (which, at that time, were not considered heroic measures), administered to stem rampant systemic infections that surely would have killed her sooner but for the drugs.

The last year of her life was a relentless, and seemingly endless, succession of one false alarm that she was in her final hours followed by another false alarm that she was in her final hours. I was called out of countless meetings to talk to her doctors. I was distracted by worry during many others. I spent several evenings each month walking mile after mile in the hallways outside hospital emergency rooms, putting my children to bed by phone. This went on for so long that I began to pace myself as though I was in an endurance event rather than at the end of my mother's life. I don't remember ever thinking about it, but looking back, I can see that I began to dole out my attention, more and more parsimoniously, as it began to look like her decline would never end.

Perhaps I worried that I would not outlast the ordeal, that I would run out of some unnamed something or other if I didn't put myself on an emotional budget. Or perhaps I became exhausted by the continual vigilance. Or perhaps I was just too scared by what was happening to stay connected to it.

My mother became unrecognizable to me. I did not know how to be with her in her growing decrepitude, so I began to be with her less. At first, I began visiting her less frequently. Then my visits became shorter. I eventually stopped bringing her to my house for dinner. I stopped bringing my children to visit her. In short, I stopped relating to her as my mom, and, instead, began to deal with her as though she were a problem, one that needed some attending—but not much attention.

When she finally died, I found that I was left with a huge reservoir of love and concern for her. It turns out that my budget had been too severe, and I am left with a surplus, all of which belongs to her. I am so sorry I did not know how to arrange myself so she could have gotten all I had.

Regrets for what was done or left undone are fairly typical of the grief after parents die. Although it is often called "guilt," in the conventional language of grief, it seems to me that it really is more a type of regret—either that we did not do more when we had the opportunity to do so or that we did not get the opportunity to do more.

I witnessed the ubiquity of this feeling recently when my mother-in-law came down with a terrifyingly serious, albeit not fatal, illness. As I watched my wife, her numerous siblings, and all of us spouses attending to this critically ill woman with such loving kindness, I was momentarily struck by how sorry I was that I could not have done more than I did for my own mother. Just then, my mother-in-law looked up and said, "Why do you think this is happening to me? Do you think I'm being punished for not taking better care of my own mother?"

The world is full of reminders of the loved ones we have lost and the parts of our lives that have ended. Some are predictable and anticipatable: death anniversaries, birthdays, holidays, or visits to favorite vacation sites. Others lie in ambush for us: We smell an odor faintly reminiscent of the nursing home and we are taken back in our memories to a time when our parents were alive; we hear a song fragment and we feel like we are children again, sitting at a campfire on a family vacation; we see hair dyed a particular color, we taste a distinctive flavor, we touch and feel a particular fabric—virtually anything can take us back and, for a while, make us remember. And for that while, we grieve, however faintly, again.

Encountering these memories stimulates longing sentiments, more nostalgic than woeful, which are grief's quietest echoes. They do not last very long. We are easily distracted from them, but while they claim our attention, we are, once again, disoriented and, ever so slightly, bereft.

I was raised in a bilingual family. Even now, after being without parents for so many years, I still enjoy hearing the music of the spoken Russian I was so accustomed to hearing when they were still alive. A few years ago, while grocery shopping, I even paused to briefly eavesdrop with great pleasure on a Russian conversation taking place in the next aisle. It felt like a sweet minivisit home, after which I was a bit sad for a while.

Memories are everywhere. Our homes become warehouses of our parents' things and minimuseums of their lives. We keep boxes of photos of people we never even knew, people they knew before we were alive. Some of these boxes may even contain their own parents' things that they never discarded because all the value was not yet out of them.

We display souvenirs of trips they took before we were born. These things continue gently tugging at us, even after they have become just more of "our stuff." Long after we are no longer actively aware that they once belonged to our parents, these mementos connect us to our past. They remind us of where we come from and who we have been, of people we have known and loved and lost.

Our parents' deaths are most commonly our first exposure to profound personal loss. Thus, our parents end their lives as our teachers—the roles they have played since the beginning of our lives. From the time of our birth, they taught us about living. With their death, they teach us about dying.

Our parents' deaths can teach us that when a loved one dies, we are left unprotected in the shadow of the primitive truths we dread, reacting much like our earliest reaction to life itself—with the frightened scream of the newborn, the heartbroken sobs of the inconsolable infant, the toddler's purple breath-holding rage.

So now to the question: What good is grief? Does such unpleasantness serve us? Can there be value, or is there only pain, when we confront such frightening imponderables?

I think there is value in the experience. I think that by illuminating life's impermanence, grief alerts us to pursue those important goals that we otherwise tend to postpone in the naive belief that our time is enduring. I think that by reminding us of the preciousness of our connections to those we love, grief encourages us to reexamine the priorities by which we have been living. I think that by confronting us with the reality of our worst fears made manifest, grief forces us to find, or develop, courage.

But perhaps most important, I think that grief—by plunging us so powerfully into the depth of our fears—teaches us that we contain much power and great depth. Despite how we feel when we are grieving, grief is not an invasion of our bodies, hearts, and minds by some external force. The source of grief's breathtaking energy comes from within ourselves.

Frightening and dramatic, grief disrupts our lives like a thunderstorm disrupts a summer day. There is always cleaning up to be done after such storms pass; old growth has been destroyed, brittle constructions have collapsed, and some hot spots may continue to smolder. And yet, as so often happens after a storm, the air around us may be refreshingly cleared in grief's aftermath. We may find that we are breathing easier than we had been for a long time. At last, and maybe even for the first time, we may find that we are able to see all the way to the horizon.

Growing Up

My father died the winter
I was forty-one.

Over his bed hung
my drawing of seagulls
sketched the summer I cried
when my fishing line tangled
in the propeller of his boat.

To support his brave show,
I did not cry in the hospital,
but concentrated on small things—
borrowed snow boots pinching my feet
voices echoing in the hall.

Cyclamen bloomed
on the window ledge,
pink against the snow,
as he held my hand
and called me his little girl.

I will never be anyone's
little girl again.

—Patricia L. Scuggs
Chino, CA

JUST EXACTLY WHO
DO YOU THINK
YOU ARE?

The Impact of
Parental Death on Personal Identity

"Personal identity" is an amalgam of all the ways an individual could complete the sentence "I am . . . ."

For instance, I might say, "I am a psychologist." Well, I am. This is a statement of fact by which I, and others, know a bit about me. I may enjoy being a psychologist or not; I may be good at it or not; nonetheless, "I am a psychologist." It is neither surprising nor distressing to hear myself say that. It is a truthful statement about me. It is one aspect of my identity.

"I am an adult"; "I am a voter"; "I am a taxpayer"; and "I am a home owner with charge accounts and a mortgage" are other statements about me that are also true. They each say something about me. They are all components of my identity.

My religious affiliation, my marital status, my age, how I dress, my gender, my taste in music, my favorite movie, and whether I'll eat broccoli or not, all taken together, portray who I am and how I am known. These facts, coupled with all the other facts about me, are all ways to complete the sentence "I am . . . ."

Being someone's child is such an important fact, from the very beginning of our lives, that it is the basis of our most identifying characteristic—our names. Each time we introduce ourselves, without even being aware of it, we say, "I am someone's child." Our names say: "I'm real. I am connected to a family, an ancestry, a tradition, and a community."

After parents die, for the first time in our lives—and for the rest of our lives—we no longer feel we are someone's child because we no longer have living parents. Changing this one fact precipitates a change in identity that is disorienting and confusing. Many of us become a little lost, temporarily. How, after all, is one to navigate when the directional beacon goes out, regardless of whether we had been moving toward it or away from it? Who am I now that I am nobody's child?

Hearing myself think "I am an orphan" for the first time really caught me by surprise. I first encountered that term when I was in my parents' house a week after burying my mother. I went there because the realtor had asked me to check on the place from time to time. I was unprepared for how strange it would feel to be there. No lights were on. No one had come from another room to greet and welcome me. The television was silent. There was a barely noticeable, slightly sweet and musty smell of mildew, old books, and dry wood instead of the customary smells of cooking. Still furnished, the place felt empty. The only sound was my breathing. And when I held my breath—silence.

I sorted through mail that had been piling up beneath the slot in the side door. The volume of offers and solicitations my father was still receiving five years after his death was impressive. Offers for credit cards and home improvement loans as well as requests from charities—eternal life, compliments of the postal service. I was momentarily bemused and mischievously tempted by the "no physical examination required" offer of life insurance for my mom.

I walked from room to room, dragging my fingers on surfaces, leaving trails in the dust. I couldn't get comfortable. Nothing seemed to have been disturbed, but everything was different. I nervously tried chair after chair. I opened closets and drawers, not even glancing inside.

The steep stairway to the second floor was narrower than I remembered. I walked into my old room, long since converted into an all-purpose/guest room. My old closet still contained some of my childhood games and even some old clothing. Remnants from an "I am" I had not been for a long time.

I squatted against the wall trying to see out the window from the same angle I had when my bed was still there. I was surprised to see how large the tree in the backyard had grown in the years since I had planted it as a teenager.

I went down to the kitchen. Out of habit, I opened the refrigerator and freezer. I saw frozen meat loaf and frozen bread from a time before my mother got sick. Taking some of each, I put them on a plate that I carried to the red kitchen table where my family used to eat meals when I was young. I sat down.

I stared without appetite at the frozen sandwich. What I was doing? I wasn't even hungry, and even if I was, who would eat a frozen sandwich?

Whose meat loaf was this, anyway? It had been my mother's until she died, as everything around me had been. But now? Whose bread was this? Whose plate was I using? Whose red Formica table? I was not pondering the legal question of inheritance—I doubted that my sister and I would squabble over leftovers. I just found it so strange to contemplate that this stuff could now belong—to no one. Who could give me permission to have some?

What, I wondered, is something that has not been discarded but rather is left behind when its owner dies? That was the first time I heard myself think that word: orphan.

Like the bread, meat loaf, plate, and other stuff around me that had been left behind, I, too, had been left behind. I no longer "belonged" to anyone in the unique way that a child forever belongs to his or her parents.

I had become an orphan.

An orphan?

I couldn't be an orphan. Dondi in the comic pages was an orphan. Little Orphan Annie was an orphan. Big eyes. Cute faces. Generous benefactors. Oliver Twist was an orphan. "Please, sir, may I have some more?" That's an orphan. How could I be an orphan? I was not a child.

But there was no longer anyone who would ever again claim me as their child. No longer was anyone living who had been present at my birth, who had witnessed my first steps, heard my first words, walked me to my first day of school, or paced the floor, nervously, the first time I borrowed the family car. No one who knew the details of my life and my family's history. I was no longer anyone's child.

All of us—the meat loaf, the bread, the plate, the table, the dining room, the house, me—nobody's.

I didn't particularly "feel like an orphan," a phrase I'd heard people use when they are estranged from living parents. I didn't particularly feel "like" anything at all. What I felt was afraid.

And that was puzzling. Why would I be frightened? Why would I feel so strangely unprotected? I had been on my own, supporting and taking care of myself, since my adolescence. My parents had neither provided for me nor protected me for many years. In fact, for the previous six or seven years, they had been dependent on me to help make decisions and arrangements. Nonetheless, I felt strangely and suddenly unprotected.

Changes had occurred before in my life. Going from "I am a first-grader" to "I am a second-grader" had not been particularly disruptive. I must have felt prepared to become a high-school graduate because when "I am a high-school graduate" happened, it was no great surprise. "I am married." "I am a driver." Transitions, to be sure, just not huge surprises.

"I am an orphan" was unlike any change I'd known.

Throughout our lives, our identities are continuously forming, organizing, and reorganizing. At first, our identities, interests, and preferences are influenced entirely by the attitudes, tastes, and traditions of our parents. Later, and at various stages of our development, our identities, interests, and preferences are in opposition to parental opinions and beliefs. "I am just like them" is replaced with "I am not like them."

Eventually, usually by the time we are adults, we have created our own identity, similar in some ways to those of our parents' and unique from theirs in others.

In adulthood, parents are like the rearview mirror of a car, making it safe to operate, as we head into the unknown, by providing a glimpse of where and who we have been so we can better understand where and who we are becoming.

When parents die, the experience is not as much like no longer finding a mirror in its accustomed location as it is like looking into the mirror and seeing nothing. How is one to navigate with the unknown ahead and nothing behind?

Lacking such information, how can one complete the sentence "I am . . . "?

~

I know a thirty-eight-year-old man named Tom who lost both of his parents three years ago. Tom's parents lived their entire married lives in a small house in a small factory town in central Pennsylvania. They were an affectionate couple, devoted to family and active in both community theater and church. Tom, the youngest child and only son, was the family's fair-haired boy wonder. Talented both artistically and athletically, he delighted everyone by dancing and clowning, as well as by drawing funny pictures. He always felt deeply loved.

Tom's childhood consisted of sports and art studies. He had little interest in academics but, being smart, did well in school. Upon graduating from high school, he attended Penn State and got a degree in art. His focus was on painting, but he was a masterful cartoonist as well. His skill as an acrobat earned him a spot on the school's prestigious cheerleading squad.

Several years after graduating from college, he and one of his sisters moved to the city, about a three-hour drive from their hometown. Tom auditioned for and got the job of mascot for a major league baseball team. For the next ten years, from spring to late autumn, he spent his afternoons and evenings cavorting in ballparks, exhorting spectators, dancing wildly to the organ music, and playfully mocking officials and opposing players. Much to the crowd's delight, he would drive a three-wheeled ATV through the outfield between innings at high speed, sometimes balancing on only two wheels with apparent disregard for safety, sometimes jumping off to perform hilarious pantomimes while groundskeepers groomed the field. Several times during every game, he would go into the stands and draw delightful cartoons and brilliant caricatures with a black marker for the fans.

It was a dream job, even though the work was physically demanding. Sometimes he would lose as much as fifteen pounds, on a hot game day, leaping about in the heavy costume he wore. But Tom had found a way to utilize his personal magnetism, extraordinary athleticism, and artistic talent in combination with his flair for the theatrical. He loved that job. As far as he could tell, he was mostly being paid to play like a kid and be cute for a few hours. This perpetual man-child knew how to be effortlessly cute.

Tom wore his anonymous celebrity easily. When he wasn't at the ballpark or making appearances promoting the team, his was a leisurely and comfortable existence. With six months off each year, he was free to explore many of life's other possibilities, but he felt little drive to do so. Although schooled in and once passionate about painting, he appeared satisfied to casually pursue, instead, the easy sexual conquests to which his minor personality status entitled him. Although he still painted occasionally, he spent most of his considerable off-season spare time in a neighborhood gym exercising and lifting weights.

When Tom's mother called one day to say she was in the hospital because of back pain, Tom and his sisters thought she was probably making a big deal out of nothing. She had started complaining more and more about various aches and pains in the past few years, but she had always been a bit of a hypochondriac, so no one was taking it all too seriously.

Tom always liked going home, so he went for the weekend to visit and entertain his mom. They were playing cards on Saturday afternoon when her gray-haired doctor swept into the room. His lab coat fluttered as if in a tropical wind. Behind him, as though pulled by the back draft of his breeze, marched a cadre of nurses and medical students. Tom, the hometown boy of major league renown, was introduced to everyone by his proud mom. When the time came for the doctor to perform his examination, Tom stepped out into the hall to give his mother privacy.

He was tired. This visit seemed unusually difficult for him, although he couldn't say why. He leaned against the hard institutional brown tile wall and closed his eyes, hoping for a few minutes of rest. He couldn't help overhear snatches of the conversation from inside his mother's room.

"Yes," he heard the doctor say, "I know. The pain. You remember that I told you that chemotherapy would not prevent the cancer from spreading but would only slow it down? Well, we got eight years out of it, but it's in your bones now."

Tom couldn't understand what he was hearing. Chemotherapy? Bones? What was this guy talking about? His mother had a backache. He knew she had had a mastectomy eight years previously, but he and his sisters had been assured the operation was successful and that everything was fine afterward. No one had ever said anything about recurrence of cancer or chemotherapy.

As soon as the doctor left, a suddenly frightened Tom reentered the room, sat on the edge of his mother's bed, and said, "What's going on?" Just then his father came into the room, heard what had happened, and began to cry.

For years, Tom's parents had been bearing the burden of knowing that his mother's cancer had not been eradicated by the mastectomy. In fact, it had already begun to metastasize by the time she was operated on. Several courses of chemotherapy had slowed its spread, extending her life well beyond the early predictions of her doctors, but it appeared she was now running out of time. His parents had decided to lie about her condition all these years, they said, to spare their children the worry.

All his mother's complaining now made sense to Tom, but he was angry at having been lied to. Maybe parents need to protect their children from scary news, but he and his sisters were grown-ups, weren't they? He called his sisters, and the whole family gathered that evening in the hospital room.

It was a difficult meeting. Tom and his sisters, confused by the sudden turn of events, expressed hurt and dismay at having been lied to as well as concern for their mother's condition. The parents explained again and again how they had merely been trying to be good parents. Lots of crying. Lots of hand-wringing. Lots of hand-holding.

When their mother grew too weary to continue, Tom and his sisters went back to the house to continue their conversation. Their father stayed at the hospital, as he had been doing, in their mother's room.

This was a lot for Tom and his sisters to grasp at one time—their mom's illness coupled with their parents' conspiracy of silence. They vowed to get past their hurt, help their mother, and relieve their dad, who had been shouldering the burden of this sickness alone. But how were they to deal with the fact that their parents had treated them like children? They talked late into the night.

The next morning they met with the doctors, who were pessimistic. Their best prediction was that their mother had a rough month or so ahead of her before she would die. They could make her somewhat more comfortable, but they could offer no hope.

But she fooled them. Maybe because her children were there or maybe because of her own stubborn nature she did not decline that rapidly. Perhaps being relieved of the burden of the secret freed her to fight better. Two months later, she was getting stronger and feeling better.

That was when her husband collapsed and, in one of life's perverse twists, was found to have advanced bone cancer. No warning. No hints. No lies. Could it have been the stress of holding in a secret all those years? It didn't matter. What mattered was that the whole world, impossibly, seemed to be caving in.

Tom's parents shared a hospital room for the next month, inseparable at the end as they had been throughout their lives. None too subtly, the burden of care and decisionmaking had shifted to Tom and his sisters. Tom's responsibilities had become much more serious than merely being a parental amusement. The world had started to change.

Within the month, Tom's parents died, his mother a week after his father. Tom delivered tender eulogies at both funerals.

He did no clowning, and he was not cute. Although he told gentle stories to commemorate his parents, he felt lost and confused. He kept being distracted by the growing awareness "I am becoming one of the grown-ups."

Not only, he realized, had he and his sisters taken over their parents' place as the decisionmakers for the family but they had also taken their parents' place at the head of the line to die, a point driven home when they arrived at the cemetery and saw three chairs, one for each of them, under the tent erected to protect mourners from the rain at the edge of the grave.

A military bugler from the local VFW played a haunting taps as the color guard lifted the flag from their father's coffin and folded it into a perfect triangle. That done, a crisply dressed soldier turned, walked over to Tom and his sisters sitting in the three mourners' chairs, and presented the flag with a crisp salute. Tom and his sisters looked at each other, uncertain who was to accept this honor. Finally, Tom stood and accepted the flag. Looking around with a tear-streaked face, he thought, "This is as grown up as it gets."

He had never imagined going through something as difficult as this day without his parents' guidance. Despite seeing so many friends smiling sadly at him from under their umbrellas, Tom felt alone.

As he got on the highway to drive home the next day, this sense of isolation filled him. He noticed all the cars speeding along, carrying their cargo of passengers—people who had no idea of and felt no concern about the magnitude of the recent events in his life. He began to feel disconnected from the world. "You can be close to your siblings," he later told me, "but parents were the continent. It's like the continent sank below the water. It's gone, and you suddenly become alone, no longer part of the mainland. My sister is another island, and there's a bridge connecting us, but I am an island now."

The only people he could think of with whom to share this awesome awareness and from whom he might possibly get solace were his parents. Years later, he still gets the urge to call them to share the very terrible news that his parents have died. He wishes he could talk it over with them, as he did so many other things in the past. He misses them and their wisdom.

Within a few weeks of delivering his second eulogy, it began to occur to Tom that he wasn't getting any younger. He calculated that he was the age his father had been when he was born. Perhaps he realized that he, too, would someday die. For the first time in his life, his identity included "I am mortal."

Living parents provide the comforting illusion that it is always someone else's turn to die before it is our turn. That illusion, and the protection it offers, perishes when they do.

Because it introduces this awareness of mortality, parental death refocuses our sense of time. While parents are living, time is "elapsed time," for example, "I have lived so many years," "I have been out of school so many years," "I have been married so many years," and so on.

When parents die, life's temporary nature becomes certain. A woman I know whose mother died at the age of forty not only became aware of just how young her mother had been when she died but also began to think about her own death as she neared that fatal age. Parental age at death is a very strong unconscious predictor of life span. Most of us begin estimating our own life expectancy once the life span of our parents is known.

In fact, as a rule, people who are older than the age at which both of their parents died tend to be more aware of their mortality than people older than they are who have not yet surpassed the oldest age achieved by their parents.

Once life-span awareness has formed, time starts being considered "time remaining"; that is, thoughts such as these surface: "I am going to retire in so many years," "I am getting too old to have children," "I am going to have to get a new car soon," and so forth. Such thoughts create a sense of urgency as well as isolation, bringing a feeling of estrangement from others.

Everything starts looking and feeling different. We may feel different with people, even people we know well. We may feel temporarily unable to make contact with friends in formerly familiar ways. It becomes an effort to maintain contact with others. As the title character says in Rainer Maria Rilke's *The Notebook of Malte Laurids Brigge*, "I don't want to write any more letters. What's the use of telling someone that I am changing? If I'm changing, I am no longer who I was; and if I am something else, it's obvious that I have no acquaintances. And I can't possibly write to strangers."

This sense of isolation, of being a stranger—"an island, no longer part of the mainland," as Tom put it—is the threshold to the development of an altered identity. Before parents die, their children, regardless of age, are, at least in part, connected to the rest of the world through them. After their death, that connection is broken, the surviving adult child becomes alone in a way never before experienced, and a new part of life begins.

In surprisingly short order, after returning from his parents' funerals, Tom began to change. He became increasingly dissatisfied with how he was spending his life. The novelty of his employment was no longer amusing. He resigned from the mascot job. He designated a room in his apartment as a studio. He began painting large canvases, often containing portraits of some of the beautiful women he used to date. He told people he was committed to making his way as a full-time freelance artist.

By the end of the year, he had an agent in Los Angeles; he had entered and won a significant national art competition; and he had a show entitled "Tom's Women" at a prominent New York gallery, displaying his depictions of models and starlets, once merely objects of conquest to him, as lovely and sophisticated women.

Now, Tom is still making use of his remarkable gifts, but he has begun taking himself seriously as an artist, as an adult, and as a man. He still works out at a gym, dates beautiful women, and loves to play like a kid, but it's different for him now. He has opened a retirement savings account. He is buying computer equipment with which to develop a commercial art service. He has mailed his portfolio to hundreds of art directors in public relation firms nationwide.

Tom no longer thinks of himself as a distraction from the main event, as he did when he was mascot for the baseball club and when he was his parents' delightful youngest child. He has, literally, removed that costume and taken off the feathery mask of the clown. He now presents himself, without disguise, as the main event.

Some of his friends think he is not the same Tom. Others say he has finally grown up. But because our culture does not recognize the enormous impact parental loss has on adults, no one says, "That's what sometimes happens when parents die."

But it is. Changes in self-definition and associated behaviors commonly follow the death of parents. These changes are not consciously associated with parental death in the minds of surviving adult children. They just seem to happen. Tom did not think, "Hmm. Now that my parents are dead I will change jobs, start taking myself seriously, and become an artist." In fact, when the changes he had manifested since his parents' death were pointed out to him, he was surprised that their death played any role in those developments. He said, "I thought I was just growing up."

The death of parents represents, as it did for Tom, a confrontation with the certainty that death is not what just happens to other people. This often leads to an urgency to get on with important but heretofore neglected life goals. Important aspirations, postponed in the comfortable denial of life's impermanence, begin to take on new and compelling value. Decisions to marry or divorce are commonly acted on, as are decisions to begin having children, go back to school, begin saving for retirement, or, for that matter, begin writing a book, as I have done.

Parental bereavement, however, does not invariably precipitate ennobling transformation. Sometimes people's growth is spurred in a direction incompatible with social norms, manifested in ways that are displeasing to others. Change is not, by definition, improvement. Growth is not always in a straight line to the sun. What constitutes an opportunity for "fulfillment" for one person may represent an opportunity for regression to another.

~

My friend Patrick lost his second parent when he was nearly fifty years old. Prior to their deaths, he appeared every bit the distinguished gentleman. Courtly in manner, conservative and elegant in dress, he carefully maintained his hair color to offset its perfectly combed youthful brown with an elegant hint of distinguished gray at the temples. Discretely yet unapologetically gay, he always conducted himself modestly, lest he give offense to his straight friends or his parents, all of whom knew of his sexual orientation but may have been uncomfortable with any overt appearances of impropriety.

A devoted volunteer for causes he believed in, he was well regarded by his colleagues and well liked by his friends and neighbors. By all conventional measures, Patrick lived a successful and satisfying life.

His parents, with whom he was always very close, lived on the other side of town in the house in which he and his brothers had been raised. In addition to the five of them, his mother's two bachelor brothers had also lived there until their deaths.

Although marginal to the operation of Patrick's family, these uncles always contributed financially and were a constant benevolent presence in the household throughout his youth.

As his parents became older and more brittle, Patrick began spending Sundays with them, taking them to church and then staying for dinner. He admired his father, a retired civil servant, and he adored his mother, a no-nonsense career nurse who only stopped working, at the age of seventy-four, because of her husband's deteriorating health.

Patrick had virtually no relationship with his brothers, both of whom lived out of town, because of their being embarrassed by and rejecting his homosexuality.

After his father died, Patrick became even more solicitous of his mother. He helped manage her finances, which were swollen to a considerable sum by the inheritance from both her brothers' life savings and her husband's life insurance. On Sundays, he began taking her to visit her nearby old friends after church. He even accompanied her on a six week excursion through Ireland, staying with relatives with whom his mother had corresponded but had never met and visiting locations from which their ancestors had emigrated. This was not an easy undertaking for Patrick because of his mother's rickety condition, but he remained careful and patient with her throughout the trip, never losing his temper and never expressing his exasperation at her slow pace and failing memory. He was sustained by the thought "I am a dutiful and loving son."

Within a year of returning from Ireland, they agreed she would sell the family house and move into an assisted living facility near Patrick's house. Barely settled in her new apartment, she fell, broke her hip, and died during the surgery to set the broken bones.

Patrick was immobilized by grief for months. He would dissolve into tears, unprovoked, during seemingly insignificant conversations. He often referenced his parents' deaths, and he began to speak about his own. He purchased a nursing-home insurance policy. He lost so much weight that he had to begin buying new clothes.

It was with that emerging new wardrobe that people first became aware of Patrick's change. While in the past his taste had run to subdued colors and generous sizing, he now began buying and wearing tight and brightly colored outfits more appropriate to someone twenty-five years younger and fifty pounds lighter.

He got his ear pierced and started wearing a diamond stud. He bought a big signet ring, a new red sports car, and a new house, decorating the latter with Victorian furniture, Oriental rugs, and velvet-patterned wallpaper adorned with mirrors. He hung a large painting featuring nude young men over his new queen-size bed with brass headboard.

In the past, Patrick had always vacationed on his own, albeit often going to locations known for gay nightlife. Now he began taking much younger men on trips with him. He lavished his money generously on these often overtly and outrageously effeminate men, who cheerfully helped him spend lots of it. He invariably lost interest in them upon returning home.

Although his parents had raised him a Roman Catholic and he had studied for the priesthood while in college, he stopped attending his parents' church and left the faith. He began to attend a local Episcopalian church, where he felt less condemned for his unmarried life and sexual orientation.

Always in the past a believer in a socially progressive agenda, he became conservative in his politics and reactionary in his attitudes toward issues of race, class, and gender opportunities. He joined an elitist fraternal organization he would have scoffed at years earlier and began associating with different people than he had throughout his early adulthood. A lifelong Democrat from a family of Irish-American lifelong Democrats, whose father was a civil servant to a succession of Democratic city administrations, Patrick even confided to me that he had voted for a Republican.

He never seemed to be quite at peace with these changes, however. His moods seemed to vacillate between elation and desperateness like an adolescent's. Perhaps he thought mournfully, "Now, I am my own man."

One day, nearly a year after this transition had begun, Patrick stopped to pick up his shirts from the elderly woman who did his, and my, laundry. As she good-naturedly chided him for the amount of storage space he was monopolizing in her little shop by leaving so many shirts with her for so long, he, in an outburst heretofore unimaginable from him, exploded: "Don't you dare tell me how long to leave my things here. You don't have the right to tell me what to do. You are not my mother."

It is tempting to dismiss such changes in behavior and style under the popular and much-maligned rubric "midlife crisis" or to speculate that Patrick underwent some sort of grief-induced breakdown in personality. I would not agree.

There is a kind a liberation associated with the deaths of parents, in addition to the disorientation and sorrow they impart. When we survive our parents, we are finally released from behavioral conflict: Gone is the behavioral restraint based on loving and respectful feelings for aged parents whose approval is still paramount; gone also are the internal pressures to fully express ourselves as individuals in ways different from, and possibly even unacceptable to, our parents.

I suspect that midlife crisis, about which so much is written—especially in a particularly derogatory manner—is sometimes another manifestation of identity reorganization associated with parental death. It might be characterized by these thoughts: "I am finally free. There's nobody whose opinion of me matters anymore. I don't care what anyone else thinks. After all, what are they going to do if they don't like what I'm doing . . . tell my parents?"

Parental loss is a powerful event that spurs some toward maturation and creativity while propelling others into a regressed reclamation of unfinished adolescence. Perhaps death of parents in adulthood *is* the midlife crisis.

To some degree or other, it is certain that the death of parents during their children's midlife precipitates a crisis in identity. Life with two living parents is just different from life with no living parents, regardless of the particulars. How we complete the sentence "I am . . ." gets disrupted in the transition between these two states of adulthood.

I suspect that this transition is an echo of what happened when we were born. Involuntarily expelled from the womb, we were cut off from a place where life was as it always had been and forced to be in a place that was not familiar. Having experienced the adult transition of becoming an orphan, I can understand why birth is invariably so messy and why most infants are born screaming.

Old people say that one never really grows up until one's parents have died. Maybe so. A piece of fruit is "mature" when the stem, by which it has always been supported, nourished, and attached to its roots, withers. Perhaps that is how it is with people, too. Perhaps only after parents have died can people find out what they are going to be when they grow up.

I Couldn't Do It, Dad
(In memory of my father, David Marcus, 1905–1991)

It was Thursday and I had to
place the ad in the Trib

People who never knew you
would come to see it
Someone might buy it

I'd have to rent a new one
not drive around pretending
I was a hippie in a rundown car

The fender's rusting off
all your stuff in the trunk

but when I took it
for a smog test, it passed

I renewed your insurance
for another year

God, Dad, I'm happy
Maybe it won't become

a classic, but I'm driving
your '74 Dodge Dart

and keeping you alive
ten months after your death

—Elaine Starkman
Walnut Creek, CA

I'll Be Seeing You in All the Old Familiar Places

*Ongoing Relationships
with Parents
After They Die*

Before my parents died, I never imagined that the dead could continue to play significant roles in the lives of the loved ones they left behind. In those innocent days, I still assumed life made sense, that the universe was governed by reason. I didn't yet appreciate how much of life takes place in our minds.

I certainly thought that when someone dies, that person is dead—not to be heard from again, at least not in this world.

Had someone told me, back then, that he had been visiting with one or both of his dead parents, I might have understood him to be saying, rather quaintly, that he been thinking about, or missing, his parents. Or that he'd been remembering a time or an event from the past. It would never have occurred to me that he could literally have meant that he'd been visiting with his parents as vividly and unmistakably as if they had been there in the flesh.

As a child, I witnessed something of the persistence of memories. I grew up in a community in which most of the older generation, including my parents, were immigrants who had fled Eastern Europe during the Nazi and Soviet expansion of the 1930s and early 1940s. Virtually everyone my parents knew was from somewhere else.

Languages other than English—Russian, Lithuanian, Polish, Hungarian—were spoken in homes and played on radios. The vapors of richly flavored cabbage soups and exotically spiced stews so permeated the wallpaper and woodwork that their odors filled the houses on sweltering summer days regardless of what was on the stove. Homes were shrines to foreign lands, walls draped in faded tapestries and bookshelves lined with illegibly embossed and brittle book bindings.

In a remote corner of nearly every living room stood a small table, usually covered with a fine lace or linen runner, on which stood numerous ornately framed photographs, fading sepia images of serious-looking, formally dressed people sitting or standing in foreign places. Those people, and those places referred to as "over there," had been left many years before, but they had never been entirely left behind.

Once in a while, a brittle blue onionskin envelope, with precisely scripted address and exotic stamps, would arrive from "over there." People would gather eagerly, albeit sometimes sorrowfully, to read and discuss the news from abroad in the rapid-fire staccato of their native tongues.

I remember seeing my mother, late one night, sitting at our red kitchen table and writing on a piece of blue onionskin paper with a fountain pen that made a hollow scratching sound as she moved it across the page. She had placed one of the old framed photos near her on the table, and she would occasionally stop writing and gaze fondly at it, a tear sliding on her cheek.

These were extraordinarily patriotic Americans. They proudly paid taxes and voted in every election. They delighted in the diversity of opinion they found in newspapers. They never missed an opportunity to express their gratitude for the new and precious freedoms they found here, or to remind us, the native born, about our privileged lives.

Yet despite their unswerving allegiance to their adopted country—to say nothing of the fact that their homelands were now drastically changed by the political upheavals they had fled from—they retained a lingering connection to the land, people, manners, cuisine, music, language, and customs of their origins.

I remember trying not to roll my eyes with bored dismay as they would tell, yet again, the story of some remote relation whose picture was among their collection.

I wondered how was it possible to be so loyal to America and, simultaneously, so rooted in a different time and place—a time that was past, a place that no longer existed. I wondered why they lived like that, simultaneously moored in the past and the present.

As a boy watching the grown-ups, I could not yet understand that these artifacts, and the memories they evoked, were all that remained of the place where these people had grown up, where they had been shielded within a family of protective elders, and where they had known innocent pleasures—in a word, their home.

Everyone I loved, and everyone who loved me, was still living in the same house that I was. I did not know that this would ever change. I did not yet know that, inevitably, all of us are separated from our origins. I did not yet understand that the departure from that spot called home—be it voluntary or involuntary, be it to pursue a dream or to escape a nightmare, or be it when we step into what's next or step out of what's gone—leaves a compelling trail in the heart of the pilgrim forever.

Now that both my parents have died, however, I have begun to understand that we all become exiles, eventually. I now appreciate that, like them, we all spend adulthood in a rapidly changing culture and society in which we often feel alien. I now realize that we who cannot go home again are never entirely free of our attachment there. Who we knew, who we loved, and who we have been loved by are enduring facts that provide continuity in our otherwise changing lives.

I think we all maintain memories of those precious people we have known and loved in some remote corner of our minds, preserved as carefully as if they were brittle snapshots displayed in ornate frames, on a table covered with the finest linen or lace.

And, occasionally, they let us know they are still around.

Many people who have undergone the loss of a loved one have told me that eventually, something personal but out of the ordinary happens and, in a way that transcends the physical reality of death, they experience themselves as having been in contact with the deceased.

A few years ago, I had a client named Rachel, a sculptress. She had come for help because she had completely lost confidence in her creativity after her father died. She described the feeling as "being frozen." This creative block was becoming an increasingly serious problem for her since a deadline for some commissioned work was rapidly approaching.

One day she came for her regularly scheduled appointment and, perching on the edge of the hard chair where she usually sat, asked if she could tell me something weird that had happened. That's the word she used.

"Weird?" I asked.

"Really weird," she said.

"How weird?" I asked.

"So weird," she said, "that I'm afraid you'll think I'm crazy. And, as a matter of fact, I'm not so sure I'm not crazy."

Confident that she was quite sane, I replied, "Okay. I can handle crazy."

She laughed and sat back in the chair. It occurred to me how strange it was that I had never, really never, seen her laugh before, and I wondered what could have transpired that would begin her thaw.

I also noted, as I sat there waiting for her to start, that unlike her ordinarily tidy and well-groomed appearance, her hands were stained and her hair was somewhat disheveled. She was wearing dirty overalls.

"Well, I've met with a contractor who is going to start some remodeling on my house," Rachel said. "And I've been working nonstop on one of the commissioned pieces for the past thirty-six hours."

I remembered that in our first meeting she had told me that she had been creatively blocked in the past and that she knew she would break out of her doldrums and get back to work as soon as she could get going on something. Anything. It didn't matter what. She had said: "If I could even do something like start remodeling my house, I'd get unstuck. But I can't afford to remodel my house because no money is coming in since I'm not getting these commissions done."

Rachel stretched, got up, paced, and began: "Last Friday was my birthday, and all I could think of was that if my dad were still alive, he'd call and we'd go for a walk and talk about this terrible block I'm having. So I decided I'd go to a nature trail my dad and I had often hiked on, and I'd pretend he was with me. Pretending like that doesn't come easy to me, but I put on his old hunting jacket and drove to the nature preserve, which is only a few miles from my house, determined to give it a try."

She sat back down and was silent for a minute gazing down at her hands and picking at the stains. In a quiet voice she continued, telling me that when she got to the nature preserve, the parking lot was empty except for wind-blown piles of red and yellow leaves that had fallen from the trees and were lying all over the place. When she got out of the car, something odd caught her eye and she bent down. There, on the ground right next to her car door, were four rose stems and rose petals scattered nearby. They looked, she said, as though they had been discarded by a recent visitor.

"And as soon as I saw them, I began to sob," she said. "You know, my dad used to buy me four roses for every birthday. It felt like he was saying, 'Okay, I'm here. I didn't forget.'"

Rachel walked for over an hour, missing her parents and thinking about her current dilemma. Returning to the parking lot, still disheartened and sad, she noticed more debris near her car, something she had not noticed before.

"This is what I found." She said, hesitantly reaching into her back pocket and withdrawing a soiled and weathered fragment of heavy ivory-colored paper that appeared to have been torn from an old Christmas card. There was something written on it, in a very precise and feminine hand, that said:

[A]nd we think you are smart to fix up the living room with a wall around the duct work and paint. Why don't you finish around the window to the deck while you are doing the work in the L.R.?

Here is the other Merry Christmas check. Dad wants to add an extra amount to be sure you have enough to do all that you want to do in the L.R.

We love you always,
Mother

I looked up. We stared at one another for a few moments, and then she continued: "I drove home in a bit of a daze, as you can imagine. When I got there, the mail had come, and there was a notice to go to the post office for a registered letter. I went. The letter was from Dad's old stockbroker. He was sending me a check for $10,000. Some zero coupon bonds my dad owned, about which I knew nothing, had matured.

"So," she sighed, stretching her arms over her head, this time arching her back contentedly, "I'm remodeling my house, and I'm back to work. Weird, huh?"

"Very weird," I replied.

We spent quite a while talking about how it had been for her to feel as though she was not only in contact with her dad again but being helped by him again—and in such a mysterious way. Rachel is not at all given to the mystical, and she was at a loss to know how to grasp and hold onto that magical day.

We spoke for a long time that day. She talked a lot about her dad, their special relationship, and her amazement at the possibility of his playing an ongoing part in her life.

I explained to her that while such peculiar occurrences are certainly not part of anyone's typical day, stories of this sort are quite common among the bereft. I told her that some, like hers, involve inanimate objects discovered in strange locations and are understood as messages from loved ones. Other times, an animal is observed behaving in a way that seems significant, be it a butterfly floating past graveside services and perching briefly on the shoulder of the clergy or a hawk circling and screeching high above in the sky, with mourners knowing that the spirit of the departed is visiting.

We wondered together at the underlying reality of such "weird" events. I told her that I knew them not to be the exclusive province of parental loss because I had had such an experience and it was not associated with my parents. Rather, it was associated with another very important loss—that of my sister.

It was back in 1991, on a weekday during the hottest part of the hottest month of the summer. I was at work, having an ordinary day in my life as a psychologist. I was seeing people for psychotherapy that day, and I had a pretty full schedule of appointments. At the end of each session, I would say good-bye, then close the door to the hallway after the client left, go to my desk, make some notes to put into the record later, go to the waiting room door, and admit the next client. I had already done that a few times that day. Nothing remarkable was happening.

At eleven o'clock, I found a middle-aged couple sitting in the waiting room, as I had expected. This was their third meeting with me for marital therapy. Both previous times I had found them sitting on opposite sides of the waiting room, staring blankly at each other. This time, however, they were sitting next to each other, apparently transfixed by something in the corner of the room.

I looked to the spot where they were staring and, there on a small table, I saw a fluorescent-green praying mantis, which looked to be at least nine inches long, calmly sitting on a magazine.

I'd seen praying mantises before, but the ones I'd seen in the past were a brownish green and no more than four or five inches long, and they were in the woods—not in a waiting room on the twentieth floor of a downtown office building in a large city.

I told the couple to go on inside while I figured out what to do with my unexpected and rather spectacular visitor. Carefully and slowly, I picked up the magazine it was resting on and walked with it out into the hallway, giving no thought to what I'd do next. Not ordinarily much interested in bugs, I felt compelled to keep looking at this magnificent creature. I held the magazine up close to my face and stared at that praying mantis, and it really seemed to be staring back at me.

We stood like that, eye to compound eye, for a minute or so. Suddenly, with a familiar "ding," the nearby elevator door opened—unbidden, at least by me. The praying mantis jumped from the magazine into the elevator. Clinging to the aluminum handrail at the back of the car, it seemed to be gazing back at me over its shoulder, as the doors closed. The spell broken, I dusted off my hands as though having finished some task, reentered my office, and immediately became engrossed in the complexities of my job. I didn't give this strange interlude another thought for a while.

Five days later, I tried to call my sister for our usual Sunday telephone chat, but she didn't answer. She also didn't return my call, even though I left numerous messages on her answering machine throughout the day. I knew she had not left town; neither of us would have gone away without informing the other. I couldn't imagine where she was.

She lived alone, and I was becoming worried. I don't easily get worried, but it was unthinkable for my sister to be out of contact with me for long. I called her landlady. She told me that she had not seen my sister for a few days, and I began to fear something was really wrong. I finally called the police and asked them to help me investigate. We entered her apartment together, and there she was, lying on her bed in her nightgown—dead. Nothing had been disturbed, and it appeared she had died peacefully in her sleep. The coroner estimated that she had been dead for about five days.

I was shocked, confused, frightened, and sad. Of course I was; the whole thing was incomprehensible to me. It was impossible for me to imagine the rest of my adulthood without my sister, with whom I had grown so close after the death of our parents. It was inconceivable to me that she would go away, even unexpectedly, without saying good-bye.

Then I remembered the praying mantis. I had no association between my sister and insects. There was nothing in that experience in my office waiting room that had called her to my mind at the time. I did not yet even know she was dead. Nonetheless, as soon as I remembered it, somehow or other I knew that it had been my sister stopping that morning to say good-bye and that we had been eye to eye in the hallway outside my waiting room. I smiled to think that my eccentric sister would have chosen so flamboyant a conveyance for her farewell visit as that oversized and garishly colorful bug.

I have been told many similarly "weird" stories over the years by people who have suffered a loss. I feel quite privileged to have been told them; their impact is so difficult to convey that people ordinarily don't share them with anybody. After all, how does one begin to communicate how poignant a fluorescent-green praying mantis on the twentieth floor of a downtown office building can be or how powerful it can be to find discarded rose petals scattered behind one's car on a birthday—without sounding, well, nuts?

Since we typically don't share these stories with each other, we are left to believe that our own experiences of this sort are unique and really odd. We keep them to ourselves, condemned to secretly embracing and being embarrassed by our certainty that we have been in the presence of those we know to have departed this world.

By the time Rachel and I had finished our long conversation that day, we felt a special closeness to each other because of all we had shared. A few months later, I received a small sculpture of a praying mantis from her with a note saying, "Thanks."

There is unintended precision in calling these peculiar experiences "weird," a word that derives from the ancient Scottish/Anglo-Saxon *wyrd*, meaning "fate"—a reference to the three Greco-Roman goddesses who determine the course of human life. I wonder if such weird events might be life's reminder to us that the course of our lives is determined by forces outside of our control that we are not intended to understand. Perhaps they represent a suggestion that we surrender to whatever mysterious forces are actually running things, trusting them to provide us with what we need when we are frightened and heart-broken rather than trying to squeeze some understandable reso-lution out of a cognitive consciousness ill-equipped for the task.

Sometimes, instead of sending messages from "over there," parents actually visit, most typically while we are asleep. They appear in our dreams, and they speak to us. Such visages, very commonly reported by the bereft, can be every bit as weird as any indirect or symbolic visitation. The dreamer usually finds it confusing to encounter parents, who appear and sound younger and healthier than they remember them to be, in a dream while being simultaneously aware that they are dead.

Pauline, a thirty-year-old graduate student who lost her sec-ond parent in her midtwenties, described one such dream:

> I dreamed I was walking past a phone and it rang. I picked it up, and it was my dad. His voice was just as if he was sitting on the edge of my bed talking to me. He said, "Hi, Pauli." I said, "Dad, how can you call me." He said, "Oh, I'm around. I'm around." I said, "What do you mean you're around?" He said, "I'm around. Listen, I need a mask. Do you remember the kind of mask you wore when you played deck hockey?" I said, "I didn't wear a mask when I played hockey." He said, "Well you should have. Where can I get one of those?" I said, "Probably at a sporting goods store, but why do you need a mask?" He said, "I'm going to visit your grandmother, and I don't want her to recognize me," which made sense since we never told my grandmother that my dad died. I said, "Dad, I'd like to see you." He said, "You can't see me, Pauli. Just know I'm around." I felt him kiss me, I woke up, and that was it. Since then, his energy is always in my life. Wherever I am, he's there with me.

I had one such dream myself, but it was not nearly so well formed. I awoke with a start, very early one morning, quite agitated, knowing that I had been dreaming about my parents. I had no memory of any of the particulars of the dream except for the sound of my wailing voice echoing the words, "Not again!" I awoke afraid that there might be a terrible problem and knew that I must visit their grave as soon as possible. None of this was making any sense to me at the time, but I accepted it without question.

I canceled some previous plans for that evening and, after work, raced across town to the cemetery. I had no idea what I was looking for or what I would find when I got there. As soon as I got parked under the tree at the end of the lane, I jumped out of my car, engine still running, and ran to their grave. As soon as I saw their headstone and realized that nothing had been disturbed, I remembered the image that had awakened me. It had been a dark scene, their headstone pushed over with their engraved names face down in fresh dirt. The grave had been opened, and it was empty. This dream had so frightened me, apparently because it raised the dreadful possibility that my parents had somehow escaped the grave. The prospect that they were not dead and that I would have to go through losing them again, was, no doubt, why the words "Not again!" were echoing when I awoke.

I laughed out loud, relieved by the discovery and delighted that my parents were still forcing me, as they always had while they were alive, to go and figure something out for myself—in this case, to realize that while my grief would be unending, my loss of them was over.

Perhaps all bereavement dreams are disguised reassurance to the bereft that the loss of that loved one will not have to be repeated. Perhaps they are manifestations of our deep desires for immunity from time's relentless dominion. Whatever else they may be, they always are extremely vivid, powerful, and compelling. Those who have had them tell me that they feel as though they have been contacted from "over there," and that, if only for a few moments, their parents are, once again, in their lives.

Interaction and involvement with parents after death is not limited to dreams or metaphorical visitations. Some people tell me that they sense parents directly intervening on their behalf when something remarkable happens, as when my friend spontaneously said, "Thanks, Mom and Dad," when the rain, which had been predicted to continue nonstop through the weekend of her wedding, abruptly stopped early Friday night.

Others have told me that they have ongoing conversational relationships with their dead parent. Those who used to enjoy sharing the events of the day with their parents may still find themselves narrating the day's events to them even after they have died. They tell me that these feel like real conversations, with opinions exchanged and points of view shared.

Still others have highly energized conversations, full of emotion, with long-dead parents. These may be arguments about events of the past that were not cleared up at the time; they may be requests for advice or counsel; they may be pleas for approval. They may be defiant declarations of independence.

Parents' ongoing involvement in our lives may be helpful or may pose problems. It may provide continuity and nourishing encouragement or may be an impediment to ongoing growth. After all, there are countless satisfying and countless unsatisfying interactions with living parents throughout our lives— sometimes our parents are nice to us, and sometimes they aren't; sometimes they're generous, sometimes not; sometimes we like them, sometimes we don't. Why wouldn't these interactions, equally mixed, continue after parents have died?

I have noticed that sometimes people work out confusing or difficult ongoing parental relationships by redoing them, reinventing their history, and maintaining a relationship with pretended and simpler parents. Some enshrine the memory of their dead parents, remembering them as having been only loving and attentive. For instance, a friend of mine wistfully remembers how lovingly her father had accompanied her to the very same bank where he kept his considerable wealth to open her first checking account when she went off to college. With great pride, she quotes her father demanding of the bank officer who opened the account, "She is never to be charged a service fee. Understand?"

I am always quite surprised to hear this version of a story I had heard, told differently, years earlier. I have known this woman for a long time, and for as far back as I could remember, she had complained about the excessive control her father, a prosperous industrialist, had imposed on every detail of her life while she was growing up. I particularly remembered her telling about how he wouldn't even let her have her own bank account until she was eighteen and on her way to college. Long ago, she had told me how humiliated she was on the day she had to tag timidly behind him while he swaggered into his bank and pounded his fist on the bank manager's desk, generally demonstrating just what a blowhard he was, while setting up her first account.

Time, and her desire for a nicer dad, had apparently changed him from a bully into a hero, as she changed herself from a frightened child into a protected and beloved daughter.

By contrast, I have also heard people denigrate their dead parents, selectively organizing their memories to preserve an exclusively negative image of them. An example is my friend Mary, a professional musician in her fifties who raised two daughters as a single mother. Her voice and movements always seem gentle and calm, the personification of "cool," which is also the style of jazz she plays and sings as background for intimate dining at pricey restaurants. She and I have been friends for most of our adult lives. She lost her second parent, her mother, over ten years ago, several years after her father's death. I witnessed as she mourned her parents, and she witnessed me mourning mine. Our friendship has been nourished and has grown in the richness of these shared sorrows.

After her mother died, Mary and her sisters were amazed by how easy and sociable the two springlike days of viewing and visitation at the funeral home were. Their mother had been part of the community for many years, and there was a large turnout of neighbors and friends. Mary and her sisters, none of whom lived in their hometown anymore, visited with many old friends they had not seen since their youth and caught up on the town's gossip.

Everything started smoothly enough on the day of the memorial service, too, until Mary walked into the sanctuary and saw her mother's ornate wooden casket surrounded by flowers in the front of the church. "At that moment," she later told me, "I felt my body erupt with an anguish which was as excruciating as the pain of childbirth. As though swept up and drowning in some giant river of hot lava, I felt helpless in the experience. I was nearly brought to the floor by the pain . . . but only for a moment. Then, as though the molten river inside me hit the freezing waters of the sea, my heart turned to stone.

As quickly as it had come, it was gone. Mary righted herself, took a deep breath, and continued her measured walk down the aisle to her red-cushioned seat in the front pew. Once seated and focused on the familiar hymns, from the beautiful pipe organ on which she had played so often as a teenager, she got mad.

From that moment and for the next several years, Mary related to her parents' memory with cold, angry, and unforgiving hatred. At every opportunity, she relentlessly scrutinized her mother's every failing and shortcoming, found her wanting, and wrapped herself in a thick protective layer of hurt and fury. She railed at her father's failure to protect her from the cruelty he witnessed her suffering at her mother's hand.

"I took a bright light and shined it on their every failing," she told me recently, "their every crime, their every misdemeanor, and I stayed angry." She continued:

> It wasn't until much later that I realized that, mad as I was, I was also surrounding myself with Mother's belongings. Her paintings were hanging on my walls, her drapes in my windows, her gowns in my closet, and her sachet in my drawers. I wore her clothes, which I didn't even like. My mother was a very sophisticated Vogue-type prim and proper woman, and I am funky. Her clothes were much too large, but I wore them anyway for a year or so, not making any connection to them at all. Looking back, it's clear that despite all my coolness and anger and unforgiveness, I was keeping mother around as much as I possibly could. I was wrapping myself in her. My anger wasn't really about all her failures. It was about her leaving me.

As those who enshrine their parents may do so to establish a base of parental support and affection previously missing, those who vilify may do so to help themselves face the prospect of life without parents, a possibility perhaps too painful to endure if parents remain loved.

The images we have of our parents may be changed by necessity or fading memory. But they become precious to us. One of my favorite images of my father is an actual photograph, taken over twenty years ago, featuring the two of us sitting next to one another on the leather couch in my parents' living room. My father is holding my daughter, who was then not yet one year old, on his right knee. She is staring up at him, her mouth wide open and her body slumped, and he, balancing her with one hand, is pointing at the camera with the other, trying to get her to look there instead of at him.

My daughter, now in her midtwenties, looks considerably different than she does in that picture. A married college graduate, she is well on her way toward establishing herself in the world of adults. She is making her own decisions and is taking care of herself with no assistance from me. When the photo was taken, she was not able to even sit up alone.

I don't look the same as I do in that photo, either. I now have creases, lines, and wrinkles on a face that then was smooth. My hair is thinner, and much of the hair I do have is gray. My body is not as trim as it was, and I wear glasses now—bifocals.

If I close my eyes and imagine my daughter and me today, I do not see the little child and young man in that old photo. Rather, I see the beautiful young woman and the middle-aged man beside her in a photograph taken at her wedding, which now hangs in our living room.

When I close my eyes and imagine my dad, however, I see him as he is in that photograph—his short and wavy gray hair combed straight back, an ever-present necktie, deep laugh lines by his eyes. And in my mind, he hasn't aged a bit. When I imagine him walking around, he still moves as he did then. When I imagine him talking to me, he still sounds like he did then.

I sometimes wonder what my dad would think about some endeavor I am undertaking were he still living. Would he be proud? Would he be critical? Would he be amused, or would he think it foolish? The dad I wonder that about is the guy in the picture holding my daughter. That's the person I talk to and who I imagine paying interested attention to my life.

If my dad were still alive today, he would actually be over a hundred years old. He would look quite different by now than he did then. His memory and attention might have eroded considerably. His movements and voice would, no doubt, have changed. He might not even care very much about complex new developments in my life. But the dad in my mind remains vibrantly involved in my life, and his opinion of me has not changed at all since he died.

I have many images of my dad and my mom in my mind. They belong to me. They are my legacy. That photograph of my dad, my daughter, and me is part of my legacy, as, now, are all those old family photographs that used to be on a table in my parents' living room. Those photos, and others that I have added of the people I have known and loved, all now hang together on a wall in our living room, the exhibit having been converted from the horizontal to the vertical as it passed from one generation to the next. I am always amazed at their grip on me when I pause there to stare at those immobile faces. They connect me to my past and beyond.

All of us whose parents have died have such images. They may begin to fade with time. We may choose to rejuvenate them, rearrange them, or ignore them. They are ours to do with almost as we wish. We can preserve them as we remember them to have been, or we can redo them to look as we wish they had. We can reframe them, change them from plain to fancy, stark to colorful, wide to narrow. We can alter their appearance, and when we do, we can alter their meaning.

But we cannot make them go away. They never leave us.

They *are* us.

Just as each season of a tree's life creates, and is permanently recorded in, the encircling layers of its trunk, the people we have loved and have been loved by are indelibly registered upon, and are part of, our being. Who we are—and for that matter *that* we are—is a product of and is supported by their continuous presence in our minds.

I feel no desire to return to the past. It is a time and place that no longer exists. I am, however, enduringly connected to my history. My parents' images—whether in photographs, visions, memories, visits, or even in familiar and subtle mannerisms I see mirrored in my children's inadvertent gestures—keep showing up, like unexpected letters from "over there," and keep me moored back there and then, just as surely as I am also moored here, now.

I try to pass my growing sense of having come from somewhere else on to my children. I recognize the blank looks of frozen politeness on their faces as they try to pay attention while I tell, yet again, the story of some remote relation whose picture is among the collection on our living room wall. I don't require their attention. I know that they probably still assume life makes sense and that the universe is governed by reason.

I also know that years from now, sometime after I have died, they will unexpectedly experience my visiting them. Maybe I'll show up in one of their dreams. Maybe they will sense me in some animal's otherwise unexplainable behavior. Or maybe they will look in the mirror one morning and see my weary eyes staring back at them from deep within their own reflection.

When that happens, they will have begun to find their connection to their past and to gather the keepsakes that will remind them of their own time and place, a place that no longer exists.

Aftermath

Disclosures of your final breath brought
out bankers scrambling
for your pocket change

then accountants scrutinized your wife's
diamond ring, tally
the net worth of your son's singing
as nil,

and pawed over your garage
and garden shed like eager seagulls
at a trash heap.

Unsatiated, your brothers ripped
open the sofa looking for doubloons
among feathers, hoping to collect

on some long-forgotten debt.
In between novenas, they eyed your children
only to be interrupted by amens.

Time passed,

and yet they were all too stupid to deduce,
the only thing you left to divide
was your dust.

—**Kathleen Willard**
Fort Collins, CO

DEARLY BELOVED

Changes in Relationships with Others After Parents Die

We begin our life as an embryo attached to the wall of our mother's womb. It's our first relationship. Not much in the way of interaction but, quite literally, a vital connection. We are dependent on an umbilical cord for nutrients and oxygen, on a sack of fluid for warmth and safety. This is our first interpersonal experience. Parents provide, and we survive.

Siblings, peers, teachers, and others may exert greater influence on our tastes, attitudes, and behavior in the long run than our parents do. People our own age, especially during adolescence, tend to have more to say about the way we act, how we dress, how we groom. But what we think relationships are, what we expect out of them, and what we know about participating in them is largely based on how our parents treated us when we were young. If it was with respect and affection, we figure that's the way people will deal with us and how we will deal with them. If, however, we are treated without regard, with cruelty, or with indifference, then that's the interpersonal language we know.

Parents bestow upon us the cornerstone for all subsequent relationships—our capacity and orientation for love, trust, and fellowship.

My parents, for instance, considered honor the preeminent feature of any relationship. They were extraordinarily principled and scrupulous people. If they said they would do something, it would happen. And if they said they wouldn't do something, forget it. My father would drive many miles to return a few cents if he discovered he had been given too much change by a clerk. When I was a little boy, that was how I understood people to be and that's how I was. It wouldn't have occurred to me to tell a lie, not because I was so righteous that I consistently made the truthful choice but because I genuinely had never experienced any alternative.

The first time I was accused of being untruthful was in a playground dispute in the first grade. I was taken aback—not that someone would think that of me but that someone would think of that at all.

Now, as an adult, I realize that people are not always as literal as my parents were, and I have learned the art of embellishment when circumstances warrant. But my first assumption with others is still that I will say what is so and that I can count on them to do likewise.

The relationship we have with our parents is more than just where we begin our relational development. It remains an important reference point for the remainder of our relational lives. "How it was with my parents at home when I was a kid" can be a warm and nostalgic memory, a precious model to replicate and perpetuate. Or it can be a terrible one, frightening, to be avoided at all costs. Or it can be something in between. But it is always where we start. And it will always be the foundation on which we build our interpersonal world.

So what happens after our parents die and the foundation is gone? Our lives change when our parents die, and this is often reflected in our relationships. The death of parents can prompt changes in the ways we perceive and the ways in which we deal with our loves, friends, children, and siblings.

Sometimes these changes are big, sometimes small. Sometimes so small, in fact, as to be barely noticeable. However, even the slightest deviation, whether it be in an attempt to draw a straight line, aim a rocket, or live a life, will result in substantial change in the path of travel somewhere down the line.

Love and Marriage

On an otherwise typically errand-filled Saturday afternoon in the autumn of 1980, I stopped to visit my father in the hospital where he had been operated on the day before. He was asleep when I got there. Despite the noise I made hanging up my jacket and finding a vase for the flowers I'd brought, he did not awaken. I figured I'd let him rest and go get some lunch.

This was a complicated time in my life. Since spring, my mother had been in the grip of some still-undiagnosed disorder, for which she had been hospitalized off and on and which seemed to be robbing her of her ability to keep her balance and focus her eyes as well as to have access to her memory and be able to reason. We had been very worried about her, and then my dad got unexpectedly sick, requiring this operation. Things were a little hectic. I grabbed food when I could.

On my way to the hospital coffee shop, I ran into his doctor. He stopped me there in the hallway among the parked blood pressure machines and food-service carts and, holding onto my arm, told me that my father would probably not recover from the coma into which he was slipping.

It's hard to describe the impact such terrible words have. My body grew heavy and cold. My eyes and mouth, dry. My scalp, numb. I got agitated. I couldn't decide what to do—close my eyes, run away, curl up and scream, or grab the doctor and shake him until he admitted he was mistaken.

I didn't do any of those things. I just went back into my father's room. Easing myself into a chair next to the machine that sighed and clicked fluids into his body, I sat there for a long time, staring at that gaunt figure that bore only the slightest resemblance to my father.

My father was elderly, to be sure, but the man lying there was ancient. My father was always clean shaven, his hair neatly combed. Every day he wore a clean white shirt and tie—and looked nothing at all like this stubbly disheveled relic in the carelessly arranged hospital gown, one scrawny shoulder exposed.

That shoulder. He was so skinny. He looked like he belonged in a picture of one of the Nazi concentration camps where much of our family had perished a year after he and my mother came to America. I pulled the thin pajama fabric back into place.

"Spared, but not from ending up looking like this," I thought, looking at his once-regal nose, reduced to two holes and a hook.

I sat there for a long time, trying to comprehend it all, but my thoughts kept veering off. I could not stay focused. My mind could not stay in that room. Neither it nor I wanted to be there.

I wanted to tell someone that my dad was dying. I needed to go home.

My wife met me at the front door of our house, and we walked silently into the living room together. She and I had been married for eleven years. We had two young children. Our marriage was pretty much like the marriages of the people we knew; lots of ups and downs. Okay, lately it had been mostly down— we had even considered separation a few times. Particularly since my mother had gotten sick, it seemed, the tension between us had been escalating. But we kept saying that marriage was about sticking together through the hard times.

I collapsed on the couch. She sat on the far edge of the large round coffee table that monopolized the center of the room and crossed her legs. I started telling her about my bewildering day, but she held her hand up to stop me. Softly and deliberately, eyes cast to the floor, she made her shattering announcement: She couldn't stay married to me any more.

I stopped breathing. "Now?" I thought.

I jumped to my feet and began to pace, my fingers interlaced behind my back just the way my dad used to when he was upset. Why now? She knew what was going on. She knew things were bad with my dad. She knew things were bad with my mom.

"Why now?" I pleaded, sitting back down, hoping she would relent. We used to say we knew we would be able to count on each other when the chips were down.

Well, dammit, my chips were down.

"Why now?" I yelled, jumping back up, beginning to pace again. Parents get old, sick, and die, I thought. That's a cross everybody must bear. But my marriage? This felt like a double-cross.

My head was exploding. I couldn't think.

"Why now? Why now?" I asked over and over, unknowingly uttering the question asked more than any other at the time of a life crisis.

She didn't answer. She shrugged her shoulders and slowly shook her head from side to side—"no" more to say, "no" way to change it, "no" sense in going on with the conversation. She stood up, picked up the drink she had carried into the room but hadn't touched, and left. All these years later, she still hasn't answered.

And I still don't know the answer. But since then, I have learned a lot about what happens to people when their parents die. And the most interesting and unexpected revelation of all for me has been that a death in the family, particularly parental

death, can be a factor in a marital rift. Experienced couples therapists and marriage counselors, in fact, know to routinely ask
during their initial interview whether there has been a recent
death in either partner's family.

Learning about its ordinariness did little to ease the sting of
my marriage's demise. Most of us don't want to know how ordinary we are, especially in our suffering.

How well anything is put together is disclosed when pressure
is applied. Lean on a table. See if it wobbles. That'll tell how well
the joints are glued. Sit in a chair, scrunch around, and learn
how tightly its pieces fit. Pull a cloth to test its threads and the
tightness of the weave. Put pressure on a marriage, and find out
what it, and the people in it, are made of.

Alliances are never permanently balanced. Ongoing corrections
are always required. Both people in a marriage must have learned
to cooperate, to give and take, if their union is to endure. My marriage, already significantly out of balance, apparently could not
withstand the added pressure these troubles brought.

Of course, lots of things can have an impact on our love lives.
Financial reversals, children, illness, job changes—all kinds of
transition points and crises send reverberations through
romance, driving people closer together or further apart. But
the death of parents brings a unique pressure to bear.

Two people construct a marriage with some expectations in
mind. Their plan, their map, is invariably an adaptation of what
they knew at home. After all, the relationship our parents have
with each other is our principal model for what an adult romantic attachment can be. Their example stands as the standard for
our expectations of love. If we perceived theirs as admirable, we
will try to emulate it. If we perceived it as undesirable, we may
vow that ours will be different. But no matter the direction we
choose, the plan with which we begin will always be a derivative
of what we know of our parents' relationship.

Sometimes when parents die, the reference point and goals change, and for the first time, our own marriage relationship can be seen and understood in terms of its suitability, not its similarity or dissimilarity to the original. For instance, being willing to tolerate anything rather than risk parental disapproval, which so often accompanies divorce, may hold a marriage together while parents are living, but it becomes meaningless after the parents are gone. Or idyllic notions, like wanting to grow old with someone, may dissolve when, watching the end of our parents' lives, we realize that one partner inevitably ends up alone, anyway. Or, for that matter, an inheritance received by one partner can dramatically alter the balance of power within a relationship. Such changes in perception of our possibilities can put considerable pressure on a marriage.

In addition, people may change when parents die—the formerly indecisive partner might start acting self-assured and demanding; the one ordinarily in charge may retreat to unaccustomed passivity or indifference; one partner might withdraw from the other in reaction to increased neediness by either partner. These deviations from the familiar push on the connection. Whenever a relationship is pushed, it is changed. If it is pushed beyond the limits of its elasticity, it collapses.

But not necessarily right away. I have known couples to remain together just to get through a crisis like parents' dying. Their need to coordinate job and child care with visiting and attending to the extraordinary array of needs of the elderly and ailing—to say nothing of the desire to avoid that parental disapproval—are so complicated that they just stay together to make life manageable, and affordable.

When the crisis is over and the demands of caretaking ebb, however, the tattered strands that were holding the couple together let go. It might appear in such instances that it was the death that precipitated the marital rupture, but, in fact, the

death merely ended the necessity of the forced alliance, releasing
the marriage to go ahead and break down.

Sometimes a fracture occurs in a relationship that wasn't in
trouble beforehand, and everyone is mystified. For instance,
Cathy, a teacher and Elizabethan literature scholar, was at a con-
vention in Seattle when her mother-in-law died after an
appallingly painful yearlong illness. She remembered that when
she was a little girl, her own mother had dropped everything when
her father's parents had died. With this as her model and without
hesitation, Cathy jumped on a cross-country red-eye flight to
North Carolina to get back to George, her husband of six years.

Everyone always said that Cathy and George had found the
rest of themselves when they found each other. George was
raised a lonely only child by his widowed mother. Cathy
brought him into her large noisy family, where he found the
companionship he had always yearned for. For his part, he provided Cathy with a quiet shelter and the permission for auton-
omy that is scarce in large noisy families.

George's ordinary Southern charm wasn't in evidence that
morning in North Carolina when he greeted Cathy's unexpected
arrival at his mother's house with a cool, "What are you doing
here?" He became withdrawn during the funeral and continued
to get even more aloof during the weeks that followed. Gradually, his detachment even extended to their five-year-old daughter—just as his mother had become detached from him when
her parents had died. This was his model.

Cathy asked me why I thought George would be turning away
from them emotionally at such a time (her form of "Why
now?"). The possible association of this change with his mother's death was not apparent to her and made no sense to her
even after I proposed it.

"Oh, no," she said. "I'm sure that's not it. He wasn't even that
close to his mother. For that matter, if it wasn't for my insisting

on it, they would have had no relationship at all these past few years."

The death of George's mother placed great pressure on this relationship. It shifted the focus. For the first time, neither George nor Cathy needed the other's help to fill in the missing portions of the maps they had acquired from their parents. Instead, each now needed to return to those maps, and they were in each other's way. George needed some distance in order to grieve the way he had learned as a boy. Cathy needed to close ranks and stand with her husband in this time of difficulty as she had seen her mother do when she was a girl. How paradoxical that their relationship began to fray because of this basic disparity in their original maps, the very disparity that had originally knit them together in the first place.

The impact of parental death is not universally calamitous to love-based relationships, of course. On the contrary, love sometimes flourishes when parents die. I have known couples that stayed together merely to accommodate the scheduling and financial demands of caring for young children and aging parents who then were surprised to find their affection and mutual trust burnished, their relationship rejuvenated by the illuminating fires of loss and grief through which they had passed together.

Or there's the example of Sarah, who wondered, "Why now?" on her wedding day as she paused in the back of the chapel on her way to the altar. A fun-loving "extras" casting director for the movie and advertising industries in her early forties, Sarah had always been close to her parents. They spoke every day by phone, sometimes more than once, and she happily spent every holiday, and most weekends, at home with them. They went on vacations together. A theatrical and musical family, they often spent time together singing, acting out scenes from favorite plays, and laughing.

Sarah had always said she wanted nothing more than to marry, settle down, and have a family, but for the longest time she only dated bad-boy types, none of whom offered long-term prospects and none of whom she would ever have considered taking home to meet her parents. Although this was not the way she wanted it, men were always separate from the life Sarah had with her parents.

Sarah's parents were discovered to have cancer, two weeks apart. Her boyfriend at the time, a strapping young hockey player, had little time for Sarah's worries. He would promise to stop by the hospital and sit with her while she visited her parents, then never show up.

People would say to her, "What about Jim?"

"Jim?" she'd reply. "Oh, please." Jim was her friend, a colleague in the business. She would run into him occasionally at social or business functions and they always had a good time together, but Jim was not someone she would ever consider romantically. She told them, "First of all, he is divorced and has two kids. That's just too intimidating for me." Jim was eight years older than she was, and he was way too settled, way too serious, and way too normal to interest her. And anyway, she kept hoping the hockey player would turn around.

Sarah's parents died within months of being diagnosed. The enormity of these losses nearly did her in. She spent weeks hiding in her apartment, eating take-out food, avoiding the phone, ignoring her mail, staring at her television—and hoping the hockey player would call. He never did.

After a few months, as she slowly began coming back to life, she noticed that her old friend Jim had been paying a lot of attention to her during her time of intense mourning. He had been calling to check up on her, leaving messages of concern and support on her answering machine. He had brought food and, occasionally, flowers. He had read to her from her favorite books. He had told her stories about what had happened to him when his parents died. And occasionally he had held her hand.

Within the year, she and Jim, the man to whom she would not have given a romantic thought in the past, began to date. They spent hours together talking. They became more and more comfortable with each other. They enjoyed watching television, going to a show, or taking a walk. And, much to her surprise but no one else's, she found that she was enjoying the two children who were coming with Jim into her life.

And now it was Sarah's wedding day. Pausing before the processional to the altar, she looked around at the dignified yet festively decorated sanctuary and compared it to what she had imagined as a child. As a little girl, she used to envision herself on her father's arm, standing right there in the back of a chapel, preparing to be escorted down the aisle. Now here she was on her brother's arm, not her father's, and her mother was not smiling at her from the pew up front.

And yet this was the happiest she could ever remember being. Her heart was full of joy. How she wished her parents were here with her. She wondered, "Why now?"

Recently, Sarah and I talked, and she told me she's figured some of this out. She wonders if she could ever have formed a mature love relationship as long as her parents were still alive. "I wouldn't have wanted anything to take me away from them," she said. "And, believe me, they didn't want anything to take me away from them, either."

She has recently realized that her being with a man had never been mentioned by her parents. "It wasn't like other mothers, who would say, 'Oh, you have a date?'" she told me.

No, my mom would say, "So, how's work?" My brother and sister caused a lot of tension in the family, so it was up to me, the typical middle child, to be the one who came through for Mom and

Dad. "Thank goodness for you," my mom would say. "I can always count on you." I think the guilt, if I had gone out and married someone, would have been tremendous, so maybe I just didn't go there until after they were gone.

And so parental death sometimes permits love relationships to begin or to move to the next level. Sometimes the relationship is enriched and strengthened. Sometimes a wedge is driven into it so deeply that it will never recover. Typically, however, the effects are more subtle. Little disappointments, for instance, not passing up Wednesday night tennis the week after the funeral to stay home and just be there, are hard to forgive. Little kindnesses, such as taking care of some annoying arrangements without being asked to, are remembered forever.

Looking back, couples often see that they got closer or more distant around the time parents were dying. It is not uncommon, when late in life someone is explaining feelings about a spouse, to hear something like, "He (or she) was so attentive when mother died" or, conversely, "He (or she) just wasn't there for me after Dad died."

Meanwhile, our children are observing these developments in our lives after our parents die, and as they form the maps of what they think their own adulthood will be like, they are incorporating what they are seeing now.

Friends

During the years I was losing my parents, I kept myself from drowning in chaos by becoming interested in and curious about the changes going on in my life.

One area that piqued my curiosity was my social life. Some of my oldest friendships seemed to be evaporating. Some new ones were forming. And while such comings and goings are part of everyone's life to one degree or another all the time, this seemed different.

It wasn't as though I had arguments with old friends and then we weren't friends any more. Nothing even remotely like that happened.

Of course, becoming single very shortly after my father died disrupted many old patterns of friendship with couples to whom my wife and I had been close. But it wasn't just that, either.

Most of my friends remained stalwart, as unwavering during my long mourning as they had been all the years we had known each other. I'm sure I'll never forget who showed up in that time of trouble. Their steadfastness secured a special bond between us.

But not everybody showed up. Many didn't, a fact I only gradually began to notice. People I had known for many years, had worked with, or had been involved with in other contexts—people I had thought of as stand-up friends—began disappearing from my life.

I became aware of this only by accident. I might call a friend, leave a message, and then, later, realize that he had never called back. And then I might become aware I hadn't heard from or spoken to him for a long time.

My feelings were hurt the first few times this happened, but then I started noticing that it was happening a lot.

Once, in a department store, I ran into Joe, a man who had worked for me a few years previously when I was running a social service agency. Joe and I had lots of history. I had taken a gamble on his behalf, allowing him the freedom to develop innovative and exciting programs for which he had the ideas and talent but not the formal credentials. The gamble paid off. His work was brilliant. His groundbreaking program was impressive. He developed a deservedly fine reputation for himself as a result. He even became a member of the university faculty that had, in the past, refused to sponsor him.

Joe and I remained friends even after we no longer worked together. We played handball together and occasionally got together with some of the others we had worked with for a friendly game of cards.

The day I ran into him in that store, I realized that he had never contacted me with condolences after my father had died. This omission seemed strange in light of our years of friendship, but he seemed oblivious to the slight and genuinely delighted to see me. In fact, he said he had heard about my troubles, had been thinking about me, and had been meaning to call to find out how I was doing. We spoke for a few minutes, vowing to get together soon, but I never heard from him again after that chance encounter. Nor did I make any further attempt to contact him.

There was no rancor. We just faded out of one another's lives, as though one of us had moved far away.

It was not just the case that people were disappearing from my life. Others, merely acquaintances before my father died, seemed to be emerging from the background.

These were not people with whom I had any established history or who needed anything of me—a good thing, since I had barely enough for myself and my children at the time. They were people I merely knew, and yet they began to seek me out, to invite me to do things with them, to include me in their lives. And they became a part of mine.

Within a month of my father's death, Terry, a colleague I had never known socially, called and invited me to a party at her house. This was the first invitation of this sort between us, and at first I wondered if it was an amorous overture, the word of my marital separation having gotten out by then, but it wasn't. Over the next months, Terry invited me to numerous events, sometimes in the company of other friends and sometimes with her fiancé. Or sometimes she would just call and ask how I was doing.

I was as puzzled by people like Terry, who came forward and extended themselves, stood with me at a time when I was so sad, so frightened, so angry, and had so little to offer, as I was by people like Joe, who disappeared.

Gradually, I came to understand that what was going on was an artifact of parental death, which divides adulthood into three distinct stages: the time with two parents, the time with one parent, and the time with no parents. Each parent's death is the threshold for the next stage, a signal to move on as distinct as the ringing school bell announcing that it is time for students to go to their next class. Those in one stage of parental loss tend not to be able to imagine the realities of people who have progressed to the next. And because those at the same stage share a common experience and point of view, they tend to congregate and become friends.

I look back now on the changes in my friendship patterns during the time of my parents' dying and I realize that the people I parted company with belonged to the group I was moving out of. My relationships with people like Joe (both of whose parents were still living), with whom in the past I apparently had just enough in common to sustain a relationship, withered when my father died, and I moved into that next stage of adulthood. Some of my friends made the shift with me regardless of the status of their parents, but Joe and others did not.

Similarly, those with whom I became increasingly friendly at the time, like Terry (who had only one living parent), were those into whose group I had unknowingly moved.

I have by now heard many other stories of long-standing friendships that dissolved around the time a parent died, as well as other stories of new and durable friendships that came into being with someone similarly without parents. One client told me that one of her best friends to this day is a former sister-in-law with whom a friendship began when they discovered that they had both lost their fathers in young adulthood. With the cohesive grip of nothing more than that single fact in common, they forged a twenty-five-year relationship that has survived and has grown, despite all odds and much adversity.

I began to notice evidence of these three adult stages in a variety of contexts. For instance, in 1985, I saw a local production of Hugh Leonard's play *Da* with a group of my friends. This drama consists almost entirely of dialogues between Charlie, a middle-aged man who has come to his parents' home in Ireland to settle their estate after his father's death, and the ghost of his dead father, a lovable old rascal called Da, an Irish nickname for "father." After sitting through nearly two hours of Charlie and Da's sometimes bitter, sometimes heated, and sometimes hilarious conversations, my friends and I went to get some coffee. While discussing the show, I noticed that those of our group with living parents used words like "fun" and "charming" to describe their reaction to the play. Those with one living and one dead parent said they found the play "disturbing" and "troubling." Those of us who had already lost both parents thought the play was "magical" and "truthful." The play we saw, and its impact on us, depended on which stage of parental loss we were in.

These stages have been confirmed over and over again for me. In fact, I notice that friends and new acquaintances tended to react in one of three ways when they learned about the subject matter of this book as I wrote it. Some people, those with living parents, would respond with a polite smile and bland, "Oh, that's interesting," sort of the way they might if I had said I was writing about deep-sea diving—a mild curiosity at best. A bit interested and altogether unafraid, they lacked conversational material because they did not yet know that the subject pertained to them.

People with one living and one deceased parent reacted quite differently when the subject of this book came up. They might respond with a sudden and disparaging exclamation, like the middle-aged woman I was introduced to at a party who stepped away from me and loudly declared, "How morbid. Why would anyone want to spend their time doing that? Who would want to read anything that depressing?" I later learned that her father had just died and her mother was still living.

Others just changed the subject, like the dinner companion who said, "Yeah, that happened to my wife last year," then turned to someone else at the table and asked, "And you? What have you been up to?" I later learned that his mother had died a few years previously, and his father was still living.

And then there are people like the electrician who, doing some work in our house last winter, came upstairs to ask me a question, saw me working at the computer, and casually asked what I was working on. I mentioned the subject of the book. He began to nod his head and absentmindedly stroke his lip with his thumb. He took off his baseball cap and ran his hand through his thinning hair, his gruff voice grew soft, his features smoothed out, and he said, "Yeah, I never thought about it too much, but everything did change after my dad died." He then told me about his parents' hunting cabin by the river, always used for every important family occasion while his parents were alive, now no longer the family gathering place. He said his family rarely gets together at all, now that his parents are gone.

People like him, those who seem genuinely interested, who are not at all threatened when they learn about this book's topic, and who usually contribute some tidbit from their own experiences, are almost always those who have already lost both parents.

Parental loss is one of childhood's most fervent and adulthood's most abiding terrors. If our parents are still living, the simple fact that someone has lost a parent may make us a bit uncomfortable around them. They become different than we are, ever so slightly exotic. However, if our parents are also deceased, those who have lost parents become like neighbors toward whom we feel indulgent and welcoming impulses.

And so our friendships naturally begin to shift as we move from one stage to another. I have noticed that in addition to jarring existing relationships and stirring new ones, parental death has one other unique effect. Specifically, I have noticed a tendency among those whose parents are dead to pursue and maintain important relationships with very old people.

These often become real friendships, based, as are all friendships, on shared affection and reciprocal needs. Old people often need to have errands run, meals brought, or transportation provided. They need someone to sit and listen to their stories and opinions. In exchange, younger adults without parents, not yet equipped or willing to assume the mantle of "elder," need the opportunity to form an alliance with someone wiser and more experienced. The elder gets to give advice and be listened to seriously, and the younger gets the continued illusion that someone who knows more is still standing protectively, guarding against the fear of assuming the "all grown up" position at the head of the line to die.

There are other motivations for such connections, as well. Rubin, one of my mother's former colleagues, visited her every week during her final years. By that time, my mother had become quite confused and could barely communicate—hardly a fountain of elder wisdom. Nonetheless, every Saturday, Rubin brought her a small bakery bag of her favorite chocolate chip cookies, and they would sit together, he lightly stroking her spotted sinewy hand, and she, eyes closed and head back on the special chair in which she had to be restrained, slowly chewing each and every one of those delicious treats in silence. I once commented gratefully on his devotion to my mom, but he declined my appreciation, saying, "I always loved your mother, you know, so I like doing this for her." But he wondered if he wasn't also doing it for himself. "I feel a need to atone for not taking better care of my own mother when she became as feeble and bewildered as your mom is now," he said. "Maybe I'm hoping that being with your mom will help me set things right, even a little bit, with my own."

His answer rings in my ears to this day each time I find myself going out of my way for someone who is old, feeble, and in need of some attention. Perhaps those of us who discovered our cowardice when our own parents were dying can catch a reassuring glimpse of redemption when we step up to the visage of our former terror and lend a hand.

There are even other motivations, like those of Richard, an ebullient forty-eight-year-old bachelor. Having no siblings, he told me that he believed he grew up "selfish," accustomed to always getting his own way. Shocked by this callowness as he got older, he found, in his father's lingering heart disease and gradual dying, the opportunity and will to grow into a more generous man, a man he was finally proud to be. He related the following story to me:

I had always been a taker, not a giver. I remember one time in particular, when I was a high-school senior, my mother came into my room one Saturday morning around eleven o'clock or so, sat on my bed, and said, "It would please your father and me very much if you would make the effort to get up one Saturday on your own, without me having to nag you, and mow the lawn."

Well, I never did get up on Saturday morning and mow the lawn. I was too selfish. However, when my father was dying, for the first time in my life, I discovered the ability to be generous, gentle, kind, and loving. At one point, I even decided to move in with my father. He was having accidents at night, and I would get up and change his sheets for him. In the past, I would have gone on a tirade: "You have a urinal there. Why didn't you use it? If you didn't think you were going to make it up, why didn't you wake me? Why should I have to get up and change this bed?" But, no, I didn't say those things. It almost wasn't me. For the first time, I was able to give of myself, from my heart. It's like I was finally able to get up and mow the lawn without having to be asked, and my father told me he noticed."

Since his parents have died, Richard looks for others to help, partly to feel less lonely and partly to celebrate having been able to transcend his earlier limitations and become a caring and generous man. For instance, he extends himself for his eighty-one-year-old neighbor, taking her shopping and attempting to have dinner with her once a week. He describes her as irritating to such an extent that her own children, who are even older than Richard, avoid her. But he reaches out to her in small ways, both for her sake and for his own.

I think it's not so surprising that we who are without parents so easily affiliate with the elderly. These old people, like us, tend to not have living parents. It's as though we have moved into their neighborhood, so, of course, we act neighborly.

The transformation from having two parents to being without parents is really the passage into full adulthood. There is a kind of secret knowledge that comes from becoming all grown up that cannot be related to those not yet through the metamorphosis. For that matter, it cannot really be shared among those who are through the metamorphosis, either, but we don't need to. We understand. All it takes is a word or a phrase for us to be able to recognize each other. It happens all the time.

It happened only a week ago when a doctor I know asked about how my practice was faring in these days of managed care, and I told her that I was concentrating on getting this book about parental bereavement finished and so was not yet dealing much with the managed-care debacle. She said, "Yeah, it's really like being out there without an umbrella when our parents die, isn't it?" And we looked at each other in a new way. We each had identified ourselves to the other, and we each knew the code.

The Family

As adults, we get to select which people we want as our friends and whom we will love. We might pick them because their personalities please us or their background is similar to ours or because we have interests in common. Whatever our reasons, we get to make these types of choices in our ordinary lives.

But not in our families. We do not select our parents. We do not have anything to say about whether we even have siblings, much less how many or whether they are older or younger than us.

Deliberately or accidentally, parents include us in a community of people, and they hold sway. No substitutions permitted.

Nor do we select the roles we play or how we are known within our families. These are assigned by our parents—unlike all other areas of our adult lives, where the traits by which we are known are largely up to us.

"This one's the smart one," parents might say. "That one's the troublemaker. And those two, well, they're the artists."

The problem child, the quiet one, mother's little helper, the cheerful one, the reader, the clown, the one you can count on, the one who's good at math, the crazy one—all of these are jobs, roles, assigned by parents. They may be accurate reflections of who we are. Or they may have little to do with our actual traits.

That hardly matters. Roles serve the purpose of establishing a pattern and style by which family members interrelate, form expectations, and understand one another. And they stick.

The "problem child" is invariably at the center of family disruptions. It doesn't matter that this particular girl would rather be known as the pretty one or the funny one, even if she is as pretty or as funny as the ones who are identified that way. The "problem child" role has been assigned to her, and it is hers. It doesn't even matter whether the disruptions are her doing—they're her domain.

The "cheerful one" will enliven even the gloomiest day, regardless of his actual feelings. He conducts himself this way regardless of his immediate preferences or how he conducts himself elsewhere. It's his job.

And the "outcast," well, we never even talk about him.

Parents fashion a family much in the way composers conduct an orchestra playing their music. What the musicians might choose to play in other venues does not matter. Parents know the score for their opus, and they allocate every part. No improvising.

And age is no factor. We can be grown and out of the house with children of our own, but whenever parents take the podium and raise the baton, each of us starts playing his or her part in that old familiar tune.

But what happens when the conductors drop out of the ensemble? What happens to the song when its originators no longer enforce compliance with the original arrangement? What happens among surviving siblings when parents die?

Joanne and her sister, Caroline, never got along with each other. Joanne, younger by three years, always hated the way Caroline treated their mother. Even as adults, Joanne would pull Caroline to the side and berate her for being inconsiderate of mother's feelings or impolite around mother's friends. Caroline, in turn, always considered her younger sister a bit sanctimonious. She thought everyone would be better off if Joanne minded her own business and left their mother to attend to herself. She resented Joanne's posing as the one concerned with mother's feelings or welfare. "Hell," she once told me, "I was close to mother for years before that self-appointed moral compass showed up."

But Joanne was not "self-appointed," and both she and Caroline knew it. Their mother had labeled Caroline "the selfish one" very early, and she had referred to Joanne as "my little champion" since she was born. Neither sister had volunteered for the roles they were in.

As adults, they were never together other than at their parents' home on family holidays. They had little in common with each other, barely knew each other, didn't particularly like each other, and rarely were in contact between visits. That's the way things had been for years. The relationship between them was set.

When their mother died, it began to change.

The bank that had been named executor in their parents' will began making expedient decisions contrary to both women's understanding of their parents' wishes. For instance, the trust officers announced that they were preparing to sell off household goods at a garage sale without first having given family friends the opportunity to make selections of keepsakes.

"I know how little these things will bring at a sale," Caroline told me. "I've been to lots of garage sales, and buyers get stuff for next to nothing. The bank isn't doing this to get money for the estate. They're just trying to get everything wrapped up as fast as possible. Mom and Dad would never have wanted that."

The sisters agreed (the first time that had happened in either of their recent memories) and joined forces. They hired a lawyer and forced the bank into court, where a judge agreed that the opinions of the heirs about the wishes of the deceased had to be considered in the disposition of an estate.

Both sisters have since told me that a much more important outcome of this joint effort, however, was that they began talking to one another for the first time without involving their parents. By comparing their opinions of what their parents would have wanted, they began sharing perceptions of their parents. They discovered that a much more solid foundation of common ground existed in their mutual experience and their shared loss than either had ever suspected. They began to share memories of family events. They started laughing and crying together. They started feeling like sisters.

They began bringing their families together for special events and holidays. Gradually, over the next few years, each took on new and different roles relative to the other. Joanne became the "champion" to all of Caroline's children, teaching them to stick up for themselves in disputes at school as well as with their friends, but never with their mother. Caroline has become the family archivist. She maintains the family stories, recipes, and kinship information so that her sister and all their children can readily find out about the family traditions and ancestry.

Of course, life is full of transitions that are disruptive. Graduating from school, getting married, having babies. All of them are complicated. All of them are characterized by conflict between strong desire for things to remain how they were, on the one hand, and the powerfully attractive prospect of something new and exciting starting to happen, on the other.

Typically, however, someone is in transition, and the rest of the family plays a supportive part. A sister gets married, the others are her attendants. Someone graduates, the rest of the family is in the audience.

But death of parents is different—unique—because when parents die, everyone in the family is going through the same transition at the same time. No one is standing clear of the fray, offering assistance. Everybody is involved. Everybody feels lost. No one is spared. Everybody is looking for some guidance, and this time they don't have parents to turn to.

Disruption becomes chaos, a type of chaos similar to when an orchestra keeps playing after the conductor has left. Each participant may still know his or her part, but no one knows when to begin or when to stop. No one keeps time. But eventually, everyone starts to improvise, trying to figure out some new tunes.

After parents die, the family members have to figure out quite a bit and make a lot of decisions. They must figure out what to do with their parents' legacy. The division of things and money is usually the most straightforward. Most parents leave wills that spell out their wishes. Even the presence of a will, however, does not guarantee simplicity.

Money is easy to divide because it is inherently mathematical and therefore divisible. However, inheriting money from parents is not always as simple as making an unearned deposit of "found money" to a bank account and then deciding how to spend it. For some, inheriting money may be a greater burden and obligation than a blessing, perhaps because what might otherwise be considered "good fortune" comes at the high and confusing cost of parental death. For others, inheritance is a windfall, a blessed relief from crushing financial pressures or an opportunity to pursue some heretofore unattainable desire for which they feel grateful to their parents. And if one sibling feels conflicted while the other happily begins to spend the inheritance, tensions form.

Janice told me of her astonishment when she called her brother to tell him of her judicious investment of the money she was left by their frugal mother and he told her that he had just that moment stenciled their mother's name on the stern of the cabin cruiser he had purchased with his share of their mother's money.

The distribution of parental belongings can be an opportunity for generosity or it can become a point of contention. Sometimes old jealousies emerge, new alliances are created, and the "stuff" becomes a symbolic battlefield for resolving claims on parental affection.

What constitutes sentimental memorabilia, as opposed to trash, when a family sorts through things may be quite a mystery to an outside observer. I have witnessed siblings getting into heated squabbles over the disposition of such apparently trivial items as ancient, but not "antique," bottle openers or cake servers. Of course, things like this carry precious memories of more innocent times, when parents were still living and involved in picnics, birthday parties, and Saturday night pizza in clean pajamas in front of the television after baths when we were young. But these things also carry symbolic meaning. Whoever gets the cake server may feel that this finally confers the right to an undisputed claim on being "mother's little helper."

There are other ways that the decisions about who gets what may be translated into the assignment of new roles. For example, in one family I know, everyone agreed that the oldest brother should have their parents' dining-room furniture, which represented his informal and unstated designation as new leader of the family and host for family holidays.

The ordinarily difficult process of going through parents' things sometimes becomes suddenly and dramatically much more complicated if something surprising is uncovered. I know of one such discovery from a man who came to me for help after finding a pile of pornographic magazines, some depicting acts of depravity involving children, piled in the back of his father's closet. He felt cursed for having found them. Their impact extended beyond his own feelings about his dead father and into his relationships with his siblings and cousins, who simultaneously denounced his discovery and him for having made it.

Such discoveries can have profound interpersonal consequences even for only children. For instance, there's Anna, who
had always been considered a "poor relation" by her large
extended family. Her father had abandoned her and her mother
when Anna was quite young, and her mother, to whom she
always had considered herself close, had been forced to eke out a
modest living as a secretary. Anna chafed at the "kindnesses"
and "generosities" of her more affluent aunts and cousins, but
she was accustomed to them. And they never seemed to bother
her mother.

Nearly forty when her mother died, Anna spent months
avoiding the mundane details of her mother's estate, of which
she was sole beneficiary. Finally, she opened her mother's safety
deposit box and was astonished to discover hundreds of stock
certificates.

She eventually learned that her mother had become a player
in the financial markets with her employer's guidance and had
discovered that she had quite a knack for it. Although she had
continued living modestly, she left her daughter a portfolio val-
ued in excess of $5 million. Imagine becoming an orphan and a
millionairess at the same time! Imagine how that discovery
altered her relationships with her aunts and cousins, now *her*
"poor relations," whose past kindness and generosity she could,
and did, happily repay.

Such discoveries, obviously, can create discord in all the relationships within a family—and I wonder if that's why the things
we must search through are called our parent's "effects."

But even in families that make no such unsettling discoveries,
much will change. Traditions evolve as the new generation takes
over. For instance, there's the story Lisa told me about how she
and her brothers stopped going to church on Christmas Eve.

Midnight Christmas Eve service had been the tradition since
they were kids, handed down from their father's family. But their

father had died that year, and no one really wanted to go. They all had young children and had to get up so early on Christmas morning. Getting a good night's sleep seemed so much more desirable than getting dressed up and going out so late. But no one dared bring it up. Much to everyone's private dismay, there they were again, together for Christmas Eve and getting ready to go to church just as they had when their father was still living.

An hour before they were all to leave for church, Lisa's sister-in-law decided that her dress was too wrinkled from the suitcase to wear to church. "You should have seen us," she told me, "racing around, searching for the iron, the ironing board, figuring out where to put the water so it would make steam, arguing about whether steam or a dry iron would do the better job of pressing out the wrinkles in that fabric, and on, and on."

Pretty soon everyone agreed it had gotten too late to get to the midnight service on time, and the seeds of their new Christmas Eve tradition—staying home and going to bed early—were sown.

In this gradual and clumsy way, families reorganize and reconstitute themselves after parents die. At first it may be a bit cacophonous as each member of this once-synchronized and well-orchestrated clan selects and learns new parts. But eventually a new tune emerges.

As new information develops and new traditions evolve, new roles form. The relationships among surviving family members begin to realign and be redefined. A once-favorite older brother may come to be perceived as arbitrary and tyrannical as he performs in his role as executor of the parents' will. One formerly aloof sister may become completely estranged, the family outcast, while another may become the maternal child-care center. A heretofore annoying younger sibling may become everyone's sought-out companion. And the problem child may become the family leader.

In my friend Carley's family, for instance, she stopped being the "worrier" after her parents died and, instead, took over her mother's role of being the hostess for formal family gatherings. Her three sisters each became, respectively, the information clearinghouse, the gardening expert, and the person who calls to remind everyone else about upcoming birthdays and anniversaries, all roles their mother had previously performed.

My sister and I were not particularly close when we were younger, a function of our age difference and our always being in different life stages as we were growing up. She was six years old, just entering first grade, when I was born. She entered high school when I was entering elementary school. She'd already been out of school for some time when I got to college. We had little in common, different interests, friends, and goals. I was not particularly involved in her life, nor she in mine.

When our parents came to the ends of their lives, however, she and I were, for the first time, at the same life stage at the same time. We had to learn to cooperate and solve problems together, ranging from decisions regarding our mother's care to the disposition of our parents' belongings. We took an active interest in one another for the first time. She became much more involved in my children's lives than she ever had been, actively becoming their "aunt." She and I became companions, doing things together, like the time we decided to bake cookies on our first parentless holiday, employing our shared memories of our mother's traditional recipes. Along the way, as we got to know each other, we became friends.

And so gradually the orchestra regroups. With the addition of some new parts, the elimination of others, the inclusion of new members like spouses and children, and the loss of others who drop out along the way, a newly defined family dynamic evolves.

The baton is passed. The song—now revised and rearranged but still echoing the eternal music of all time—plays on.

Violet's Come Winter
(A Lamentation)

You can't be just gone.
I remember every thing
about your beauty.

You can't be just gone.
Where in the hell
did you go—where?

You can't be just gone.
Are the angels blind?
I miss you so!

You can't be just gone.
  —David A. Marsteller
    Eugene, OR

OUR FATHER,
WHO ART IN HEAVEN

Parental Death, the Eternal,
and the Divine

A woman grieving the loss of her parents once told me, "Now, for the first time, there is no one standing between me and God." At the time, I understood her to mean that she was next in line to die and, thereby, meet God. Maybe that is what she meant. But now that my own parents are gone, I wonder if she may have been talking about something else entirely.

I have noticed that people often go through a time of religious turmoil after their parents die. I have seen people switch denominations within a religion. I have seen people convert to an entirely new religion. I have seen all belief in a loving and merciful God shattered by the protracted suffering of dying parents, faith vanishing in a cloud of outrage and despair. I have seen the formerly disinterested become devout.

Is there an association between the end of our parents' lives and how we hold the mystery of our own? How we celebrate its wonder? What we do to manage the countless nameless terrors that are part of a thinking person's universe?

What do our parents have to do with God?

As children, our parents introduce the concept and the very name we first come to know as Almighty—be it by the Christian name "God," the Muslim "Allah," the Jewish "Adonai," the Sikh "True Name," the Shinto "Amaterasu," the Hindu "Brahma," or the Zoroastrian "Ahura Mazda." Parents decide whether the family is to practice a religion, in what tradition, and with what degree of orthodoxy. They decide which ceremonies and celebrations to observe and how much of the family's attention to devote.

If our parents considered a religious education important, we got one. If they regularly attended worship services, so did we. If they never attended services, if they did not believe in God, if they never prayed—neither did we. If they said grace before meals or vespers at bedtime, we grew up thinking that prayer precedes food and sleep.

Whenever they prayed, however they prayed, that's when and how we prayed, and their prayers became ours.

When I think of my earliest introduction to religion, I think of my father, a man so intensely shy and private that he was virtually inaccessible. He rarely gave voice to his inner thoughts or concerns. For that matter, he rarely spoke at all except to occasionally and unilaterally make an announcement as to how things were to be or to less occasionally erupt in an outburst of uninhibited fury when something, no matter how trivial, displeased him.

"*Durak!*" (a Russian word of vulgar derision, similar to "idiot" in English) he would scream at some perceived transgression, his face purple, veins popping out. And then I'd get the silent treatment—for days. That was my dad.

There were only three things about my father that I knew for certain: First, that he loved my mother. In his late thirties when they married, his affection for her was unwavering. He held her in the highest regard and always treated her with courtly respect.

Second, he thought mathematics and physics were the most interesting and worthwhile undertakings imaginable. He held advanced degrees from universities in Germany and Poland that he attended during the 1920s and 1930s. After he retired from his job as an industrial physicist, he would sit for hours in the small room of our house that he used as a study, contentedly reading brittle old books, their pages filled with formulas, equations, and charts. He appeared to read these hieroglyphics, completely incomprehensible to the rest of us, with the ease and familiarity of a scholarly rabbi perusing the ancient Hebrew of the Dead Sea scrolls.

Third, he considered anyone who believed in God a superstitious fool. He thought any compliance with religious doctrine was a sign of stupidity. He was as virulently antireligious as he was unreservedly proscience.

I don't know why he so loathed religion or why he held those who worshiped in such contempt. The closest he ever came to explaining his aversion to the faithful to me was with a quote he attributed to the astronomer Johann Kepler, who, when asked by Emperor Rudolph II of Prague why there was no mention of God in his treatise on the movement of heavenly bodies, replied, "God is a hypothesis I do not need to make."

But my father's attitude toward religion was overtly and vociferously hostile, much more than anything called for by something so innocuous as an unneeded inference.

Perhaps his faith in an orderly universe governed by the elegant and discernible rules of mathematics allowed no other dogma. To him, mysteries were merely equations not yet formulated. Either he could make sense of something or it was nonsense.

Or perhaps, as an authority on optics, he believed that all information about light, even the Light and the enigma of enlightenment itself, would only be meaningful if it could be expressed in mathematical notation.

Or perhaps it had something to do with the fact that so many members of the huge family he so deeply loved—his father, brothers, sisters-in-law, nieces, nephews, cousins, aunts, uncles—were all killed by Lithuanian Nazis shortly after his emigration to America. Killed because they were Jews. Killed by neighbors who thought themselves Christians.

Whatever the reason he so deplored religion and despite the fact that my mother was raised in an orthodox home, ours was not an observant family. We celebrated no holidays, and our house had no religious artifacts on display. I remember my mother taking my sister and me to a synagogue a few times when we were quite young, but we were never connected to a Jewish community.

Consequently, as a boy, I had little sense of religion. I knew that religion played a part in other peoples' lives. Friends of mine went to church with their families. They attended Bible study or went to special classes to learn catechism. But religion occupied no time in my life. My father thought it was stupid, so I did, too.

As a youngster, I never concerned myself with wondering what life was all about, where everything came from, how I got here, where I was heading, whether there was anything beyond what I could see and hear, or whether any superior power was running things. I considered such concerns folly, just as my father did. Religion only became worthy of attention occasionally, invariably when I got into some bewildering difficulty because I was a Jew growing up among non-Jews. For instance, there was the way I found out I was Jewish.

I grew up in a densely populated urban neighborhood on a street lined with brownstones, each of which contained three or four apartments. Bruce lived next door. He and I were the same age. We walked to school and back every day together. We were in cub scouts together. We played together all summer long. We were inseparable friends and companions.

When I stopped for him on the way to school one winter morning, I saw a small evergreen tree standing in their living room.

"What's that?" I asked.

His mother smiled, then asked if I'd join them later that evening while they decorated their Christmas tree. I didn't know what that meant, having neither heard of Christmas nor seen a tree in the house before, but I agreed to go because, well, he and I always did everything together.

What I witnesses that evening was magical. I watched that puny evergreen transform into the most beautiful thing I had ever seen. Lights and pretty balls of color, surrounded by slivers of shiny tinsel, which they taught me to carefully drape on the end of each branch, combined with the sticky fragrance of fresh pine sap darkening my fingers, to say nothing of the deliciously sweet cookies we munched—oh, it was just more than a small boy could contain. I ran home, dizzy with joy, and, barely able to speak for the excitement, told my parents about this amazing and splendid thing, this Christmas tree, which the neighbors had in their living room.

I asked if we could get one, too.

"We don't have Christmas trees," my mother replied, icily.

"I know, but we could, couldn't we?" I asked.

"No, of course we couldn't," she said.

"Why not?"

She sighed the universal weary sigh of a parent. "Because," she said, "Jews don't have Christmas trees."

Crash!

I don't think I had ever heard the term "Jew" before. This was the day I learned I was one. This was the day I learned we were not permitted to bring a small tree into our house and decorate it with lights, colorful balls, and tinsel and make it beautiful.

This was my first formal religious instruction.

I received comparable lessons sporadically through my childhood and early teens. For instance, there was the time I came home bloodied and with a broken nose after having to defend myself when a neighborhood boy, one of those churchgoing fellows, attacked me.

While she was washing the blood off my face to assess the damages, I asked my mother, "What's a kike?"

"Where did you hear that word?" she asked.

"The kid who jumped me called me a 'dirty kike.' What's a kike?"

My father, standing in the bathroom doorway, already wearing his coat for yet another trip to the doctor's office for some emergency repair to his still-skinny son, asked, "What did he call you?"

"A dirty kike," I answered.

He began to laugh. My mother and I turned in his direction, wondering what was so funny.

"Maybe you should bathe more often," he said.

Religion just wasn't hospitable terrain for me. Because we were not part of a community of Jews, I never learned that religion offers the benefit of being included in something. Because my father said religion was poppycock, I grew up thinking religion was poppycock, but I further associated it with disappointment, prohibition, and rejection.

It never occurred to me that religion could have value. My father said it didn't. Whatever parents tell us about the gospel when we are children is, well, gospel.

But parents do more than merely introduce us to a religion. To children, parents have always been there, and they appear to know everything that can be known. They hold the power of life and death. Parents personify timelessness, omniscience, and omnipotence—the very stuff of faith.

Parents know how everything works, how everything got the way it is, what is worth doing, and what must be avoided. Parents know about things that happened before we were born.

Parents are our personal "forever."

Parental characteristics serve as the model for our first image of the divine. Philo Judaeus, a Jewish philosopher who lived in Alexandria in the first century A.D., said, "Parents are to their children what God is to the world. Just as He achieved existence for the nonexistent, so they, in imitation of His power, so far as they are capable, immortalize the race."

Parents' judgments of us, approving as well as disapproving, shape and form our lives as surely as the lives of the people in any religious story get shaped and formed by pleasing or angering the central deity in that lore. Prayers for indulgences or mercy to the Almighty mimic entreaties to parents for favors and privileges. Like the Lord, parents giveth and parents taketh away.

Our parents are our Original Couple, god and goddess of our personal cosmology. They serve as model for any subsequent deities, gods, goddesses, or transcendent natural forces to which we become devoted. Whatever they may eventually be called, all personifications of the divine begin from images we have of our mom and dad.

I think back, now, on how I regarded my father when I was young. He certainly was the ruling deity in our house. Ironically, he also bore a rather striking similarity to the Old Testament God of the Hebrews I learned about later in my life, the God he so earnestly rejected—intensely private to the point of being virtually inaccessible, rarely giving voice to inner thoughts or concerns except when unilaterally declaring how things were to be, displaying occasional outbursts of uninhibited fury when displeased.

It must have been confusing for me as a child to have the supreme being in my life hold that there was no such thing as a supreme being. But that's what he said, so that's what I believed, and that's where I began my religious development.

Whatever parents teach is where the spiritual journey begins—and this is true for children who have Christmas trees as well as for those who do not, children of nonbelievers as well as children of clergy. Whatever map parents present is the map we use when we first travel.

And then comes adolescence. We begin to venture out a bit, standing apart from our parents, to experiment on our own with some ideas and begin figuring out what we are, what we think, and what we value.

I remember, as a teenager, becoming curious about this thing called "faith." By my late teens, around the time most of my friends who had received formal religious upbringing were testing their family's traditions and customs by beginning to experiment with atheism, agnosticism, or exotic faiths like Zen Buddhism or Hare Krishna, I, the son of an ardent atheist, had begun to wonder about religion.

For the first time, I began pondering life's purpose, where we were before we were born, what happens after we die, and the importance of living an ethical life even though so many unscrupulous people seemed to have such good fortune. I even wondered how people of faith could place such confidence in, and surrender to, the unknown, intangible, and unprovable.

I couldn't stop thinking about it. The only way I knew to talk about it, however, was the way my father talked about it, so that's how I began. I would provoke arguments with the devout, audaciously declaring their beliefs primitive, offering to clarify their thinking, daring them to prove me wrong. I'm embarrassed to remember once explaining to a very kindly priest how foolish I thought it was for anyone to believe in something that could be neither seen nor touched. The arrogance of youth!

Amazingly, no one broke my nose during this, the polemic period of my spiritual development. In the process of debating the faithful, however, I met and became friends with quite a few delightful and, obviously, tolerant people. Our conversations piqued my interest, so when I was in college, I took a course in world religions. On some level I expected to find it preposterous, as my father would have, but I didn't. I found it fascinating.

It was amazing for me to realize that spirituality was not the exclusive domain of the ignorant. I learned that people all around the world have similar needs and desires which cause them to they crave religious affiliation—to be a part of something larger than themselves, to express reverence aloud in ritualized ways, and to extol and worship something divine, whatever they might call it. I was quite astonished to learn that so many people, really smart people, paid so much attention to questions that, when I was a child, I had been led to believe were the exclusive province of the unimaginative or the pathetic.

The more I learned, the more interested I became. Interested, intrigued, fascinated—even amazed. But never emotionally involved.

It all stayed conceptual. I would *ponder* whether there was more to life than the objectively measurable; I *suspected* there were dimensions that exceeded human capacity for knowledge and understanding; it began to make *sense* to me that if so much of the world's population believed in the existence of some creative power beyond human comprehension, there must be something to it; but I didn't *feel* much about it one way or the other. It never occurred to me that I, too, needed to be a part of something larger than myself, needed to express reverence aloud or worship something divine.

The only actual feeling I could identify was a kind of shame. It felt wrong to be spending time on this stuff, as though I were engaged in some forbidden pursuit. I knew my father would not approve.

So, like my friends who had secretly stopped going to church, I concealed my curiosity about spirituality. I never discussed it with my friends, and, for sure, never mentioned it at home. I was intrigued by all of it, surprised by my open-mindedness, and scared I'd be found out.

I therefore never became a participant. As I got older, finished my schooling, and took on adult responsibilities, I still occasionally attended religious services but merely because they interested me. I went to all types—Catholic masses, Zion Baptist revivals, Buddhist chants, Friends meetings, Jewish and Protestant services. But I always attended as an interested outsider, watching and hearing "them" sing and pray as I might watch bees dancing in their hive. I never wanted to get too close. I didn't dare. It felt dangerous. Too easy to get stung.

What if a Jew were discovered in a Christian church? I was never clear whether Jews were welcome.

It was even worse when I was in a synagogue. There, among Jews, I was supposed to feel at home. But I didn't. I worried about being found out there, too. What if someone said something to me in Hebrew, a language I did not understand? What if someone asked about my plans for an upcoming holiday and I didn't know whether I was supposed to be fasting or having a fancy meal. What if someone asked about the bar mitzvah that I never had. Even though I could recognize some of the songs from the times I went with my mother all those years ago, I never sang along.

I had reached a spiritual plateau. Many of my friends seemed to have reached a spiritual plateau around the same time. The reaching, the searching gave way to more temporal pursuits:

jobs, laundry, mortgages. It was as if we had our spiritual selves sufficiently defined: We were either like our parents or we were not.

While parents are living, they remain the reference point for our theology. They are still our Original Couple. Our Immortal Ones. We might accept their beliefs or altogether reject them, but it is still relative to their beliefs that we have defined our own.

But eventually, parents die. First one, then the other.

The Original Couple is gone.

We lose our blueprints for God. "Forever" merely becomes a word inscribed on a headstone across town.

This is when our spiritual journey may restart and go careening off the map. We run out of answers, or the ones we've been using stop working. Whatever we've been taught about the eternal and the divine, as well as what we have decided on our own, is finally tested. This is when we may find out what we really believe—and what else we believe, too.

Sam, a professor of engineering at a nearby university, told me that he had been with his mother during the afternoon of the day she died but they had argued, exchanging unusually harsh words, and he, enraged, had stormed out of her house. By dinnertime, she was dead.

For months, he felt terrible that their last words had been so unpleasant. What an awful final memory. He told me that at first, he was angry at her for dying before they had a chance to make up. But then he started wondering if her dying just then might not have had some point. It got him thinking about meaning and purpose, life's purpose, an idea he hadn't considered since he was a little boy, when his parents would lecture him about being selfish, telling him that God put us here to help others, not ourselves. Back then he thought they were crazy. Of course, life's purpose was to take care of oneself. One just had to look at the animal kingdom to know the truth of that. Why shouldn't he take care of himself first and foremost?

And he had. In fact, he describes himself as always having been self-indulgent. He lived life in the fast lane, using up lots of things and lots of people, with plenty of recreational drinking, drugs, and sex.

He began rethinking life's purpose, and he wasn't so sure he had been right. He started praying for guidance, something he hadn't done since he was small. He returned to reading the Bible, another something he hadn't done for years. He kept rereading the Book of Esther, the story of a woman who lived her life for others. He found a passage somewhere else that said, "I will not leave you as orphans," which moved him to tears. He went back to church. Soon he was going every Sunday. After a few months, he was going three evenings a week to help prepare meals for the shelter the church runs for temporarily homeless women.

"I feel clean now," Sam told me. "Cleaner than ever." He wishes he had reformed his life before his mother had died. But he also believes that his mother's death was what got his attention, the disruption that made it possible for him to slow down, come clean, and get back to God.

Religious disruption caused by parental death is no respecter of titles or specialized knowledge. People from all walks of life, all levels of sophistication, and all degrees of religiosity may find themselves outside the limits of formerly satisfactory spiritual routines.

I was at an annual social gathering in my old neighborhood a few years ago, and Bert, a man I knew only casually, came up to me and asked if he could speak privately with me. I said, "Sure," figuring, by his urgency, that he had become an Amway dealer or something.

I had known that Bert was a devout Catholic who went to mass a lot and sent his children to parochial school. In fact, I had once heard that he attended seminary for a few years after college but had fallen in love and chosen to serve the church as a husband and father instead of as a priest. I certainly wasn't expecting him to ask me for spiritual guidance. We were both probably a bit surprised when, after having walked together to another room, he turned to me and burst into tears. After a moment, he said:

> I can't believe I'm asking you this question, but the church is just not reassuring me since mother died. I'm so angry at God. I'm so lost. I keep wondering where mother is now that she's died. I spoke to the priest about it, asked him what to do, and he told me to pray. Hell, if I could pray, I wouldn't have needed to ask him what to do. I know your parents are dead, and I'm curious how you handled all this.

We stood there together, somewhat awkwardly, him crying, and me trying to figure out what to do. He and I did not have such an intimate relationship, and we were at a party. Nonetheless, we spent several hours in that room, missing the party altogether. I did the best I could to welcome him to the murky world of adult orphanhood, all the time assuring him that I had no answers for him. I told him that I doubted he would soon find answers to his question but that, in time, he might come to a new peace with God. I also told him that although I am not a clergyman, I suspected that his anger and his doubts were a new kind of prayer, the orphan's plea for solace and grace, which he was now entitled to use whenever he needed.

I did not see Bert again until the next year, at the same annual party at the same mutual friend's house, and his face broke into a delighted smile when our eyes met. "I'm still praying that new prayer," he yelled at me from across the room.

"Me, too." I yelled back.

Changes in faith can be subtle. A good friend of mine is a hospital chaplain with many years of experience working with the bereft. She told me that her faith was unruffled by the death of her parents. She did, however, notice that she began wondering what some of the phrases she had been using for years really meant. Phrases like "they're finally at peace," and "they're with other loved ones now," rather than generic forms of comfort, became profoundly meaningful to her in a literal and vivid way. She kept wondering whether her mother, a woman tortured by terrible insecurities throughout her life, was, in fact, finally able to find some of the relief in the hereafter that had been denied her during her life, what that would be like for her, and how it would affect her soul. Previously, these may have been fascinating ideas to her, but now they were something more, something true. Her sophisticated and well-defined faith became slightly deeper and her spiritual map became slightly fuller as a result.

I believe that many of us can only really come to our own personally refined understanding and make our own choices about religion after our parents have died. We can begin forming a personal relationship to the divine only then because only then can divinity finally transcend parental images.

Only after parents die can there really be, for the first time, no one standing between ourselves and God.

Only then can we find a faith, an expression of our inner hidden way of holding the mystery of our lives, which is our own and which can now be defined relative to ourselves, not our parents. Only then, having gone past the boundary of our original spiritual map, can we lay claim to whatever new territories we discover beyond its former borders.

The year my mom died, I went with a friend to midnight mass on Christmas Eve. I had gone with him before, and the service was the same each time, but this time I felt different. I still felt a bit worried, but I surprised my friend by singing along with the Christmas carols. And I had a good time doing it.

A few months later, I attended Friday night services at a nearby synagogue. It felt good to be there, too. To really be there. This time I surprised myself by, once more, singing along with the songs I knew and mumbling along during some of the prayers I recognized from childhood. I still worried there, too, and yet being there felt all right to me.

The next spring, my children and I attended a Passover seder at a friend's house. I had been to seders before as well, but this time, and for the first time, I realized—and felt amazed and happy to realize—that we were reading the same words that countless generations of our ancestors had been saying on this very holiday for centuries. And I choked up when, at the end, we uttered the now achievable dream, "Next year in Jerusalem."

I did not quite understand what was happening to me. I was being moved by expressions of faith, whereas in the past, I had merely been intrigued by them. Like the child of a diabetic who always pressed his nose against the window of the bakery but had never been permitted the goods at home, I was discovering a powerful hunger inside myself for sweet spiritual nourishment.

But I still did not know how to feed it.

I heard about and went to visit a cousin in Israel. The daughter of my father's brother, she and I are the last of our generation, vestiges of a once-huge family. Her entire family had also been killed during the war, but she escaped from the concentration camp and spent World War II as a partisan in the forests of Lithuania. Her attachment to religion is less devotional than it is nationalistic.

She introduced me to the remainder of our family, the descendants of my grandfather's brothers, who had emigrated to Palestine long before the Holocaust began. Some of them are devoutly orthodox and others are thoroughly disinterested in religion.

I began to realize that there was room in our family for all levels of faith. Finding that out gave me permission to wonder even more about my own.

My visit became something of a pilgrimage. I spent time in the Judean desert, hiking in the hills that overlook the Dead Sea, sitting on stony ledges, feeling the hot sun and rocks bake my skin. I pretended that the people from whom I descend, nomads who wandered this land thousands of years ago, were sitting there with me. We didn't speak. We just sat together.

In Jerusalem, I visited the Western Wall, all that's now left of Judaism's Second Temple. I rested my forehead upon those massive cool stones that seemed to reach to the sky. I felt their dusty coarse roughness with my fingertips, and just as vividly, my skin knew that my ancestors were there with me. No words. All skin.

Looking straight up, I could see the golden dome of the Muslim mosque situated on the rock upon which Abraham offered his son Isaac as sacrifice to God and from which the prophet Mohammed ascended to heaven, and from which I could hear the muezzin calling the faithful to prayer.

I went to the Church of the Nativity in Bethlehem, built on the site of Jesus' birth, and I sat listening to the hauntingly beautiful chants of Armenian monks ricochet around that great stone hall. In Jerusalem, I walked along the Via Dolorosa, the path Jesus walked to his crucifixion, and I sat in the Church of the Holy Sepulchre, built on the site where he died. I peered into the crypt in which his body was placed and from which he arose.

Like trying on new clothes at the store, I was checking this corner of the spiritual world for fit, and I was surprised by how little doubting I was doing. Opening myself to what I might find, I began to feel nourished.

The indelible impact of visiting those ancient holy places is now included in my emerging version of "eternal" and "infinite." Each has filled me with wonder, a profoundly different experience than merely wondering. I do not have a way to describe the impressions all this has left on me—each moment so primitive, so intuitive, so nonintellectual—except perhaps to recall a little boy beholding the glory of a simple evergreen magically transformed into a brightly lit, colorful, and shiny thing of beauty. And this time, it is mine.

I know I could not have felt these things while my parents were still alive. Their death set me free.

I don't exactly know how to describe what I now feel about God—except that I now feel something I call God. The mystics are right when they say that only through the incomprehensible can we really understand the Incomprehensible.

But my father's influence is still evident. I have no grasp of a deity involved in human affairs whose protection and intervention can be solicited by obedience and declarations of fealty. I barely knew my father, how can I know a personal God?

I sometimes wonder how my children will embrace the divine after I have died. Their father, the virtual opposite of the father I had, was a bundle of confusion around matters of spirituality, but he was also vigilant, protective, available, and knowable to his children.

Several years ago, I got remarried to a Roman Catholic woman fifteen years my junior. We pay a lot of attention to our spiritual lives, whether in a synagogue, a church, or while listening to the tree frogs near our pond at night. Whenever we attend religious services of any type, I am moved by the music and prayers, feeling a bit more like one of the bees in the hive, albeit still on the fringes, still slightly anxious, and still somewhat disconnected.

But now when I disconnect, I revisit images I cherish. I can let the sounds of the service remind me of the muezzin's droning and incomprehensible call to the faithful or the complicated chanting of the Byzantine monks. I let those sounds transport me to a wall of ancient stones in Jerusalem or to a hill overlooking the pungent Dead Sea, where I happily remain for a few moments, connected to the world, to the past, and to the infinite mystery of it all.

My wife's large family visited us about a year ago, and we all went to mass at a country church in a small coal-mining community near our home. As I sat there between my wife and her mother, both very loving women with generous hearts, I started to get just the slightest tinge of that old fearful shame, that belief that I was somewhere I shouldn't be, doing something I shouldn't be doing—that old sense that my father would disapprove of what I was up to and would find something funny about my getting beat up.

There is a part in a Catholic service when an offering is collected. The basket that was passed up and down the rows that day, somehow or other, skipped past us. We all sat there, dumbfounded. We had money in our hands that we wanted to contribute, and we were looking back and forth at each other, bewildered as to how to make our donations without becoming a distraction to those praying nearby. Everyone else probably thought the situation amusing, too, but I was the one who laughed out loud.

The person in front of me turned to look at me, and out of the corner of my eye, I noticed that my mother-in-law was looking at me, too. My shoulders tensed, and I thought, "Uh-oh, shouldn't laugh in church, *durak*."

I turned self-consciously to my mother-in-law and whispered, "See what happens when a Jew comes to church?"

"A lot of good has happened since you came along," she said.

And so there I sat, in a church with which I had no association whatsoever other than living nearby and being married to one of its constituents. There I sat, surrounded by people I did not know, listening to a hymn with words that made me anxious.

There I sat, next to the closest I have to a parent, and she was glad I was there. There I sat, for the first time in my life, feeling welcome in a house of God.

Cancelled

where has she gone   she has gone
   I look through bills, postcards of women
   in long skirts
   sidesaddle on donkeys at Pike's Peak
she is not there
   among instructions for my father's funeral
   (the evening song from Hansel and Gretel*)*
   a Mother's Day card, a sorry-I-missed-
   your-birthday card from me
   a 50th college reunion notice
   a clipping about my brother
   home from the navy in '46
she has fled
   into the library books not yet due
   and an orthodontist's bill, 30 years old
   a poem copied on an envelope last week
   another, my father's, 55 years old
   a menu from the Mound Park Hospital last May
   a card from Austria in '62
   insurance policies, report cards
   from Philadelphia, Dayton, St. Petersburg

she has escaped me into scraps of paper
   and a shaky word on the calendar
   by the telephone: CANCELLED

   I put boxes of words in the trash, or
   burn them in the fireplace
my hands ache from sorting papers, then
I take my pen and write some more words
   looking for my mother

—Ellin Carter
Columbus, OH

STORMY WEATHER

The Hazards of Avoiding Grief

Adult life is a bit like trying to be the captain of an ocean liner and learning how to sail at the same time, not knowing the trip's purpose or its destination. Each life is a singular adventure with its own measure of challenge, pleasure, mystery, tedium—and turbulence.

It is like encountering a storm when someone we love dies. Grief can surprise us, well up, and spill over us in great crashing waves, its suddenness and intensity disorientating and frightening.

We no longer care where we're headed when caught in the deluge. All we care about is surviving the violent pitching and yawing. All we want is for the misery to end. I cannot even guess how many times I have been asked by people in the throes of grief's disruptive anguish, "Can't I just take something, go to sleep, and wake up when all this is over?"

And this is precisely what many of us attempt to do. We expend an enormous amount of energy—and put ourselves at considerable psychological risk—trying to avoid grief altogether.

In 1994, members of the Jewish Funeral Directors of America commissioned a study. They surveyed 300 members of the

American Psychological Association for their opinions about the value of graveside services for mourning survivors. The study concluded that graveside services were, in fact, beneficial for mourners, but it also produced a surprising and rather bleak finding: Fully 30 percent of the people who consult psychologists are suffering from unresolved grief over the death of a loved one. That's not 30 percent of people who consult psychologists for help with grief-related problems. It's 30 percent of all people who consult psychologists for any reason.

The results of this study match, perhaps even understate, my experience as a psychologist in private practice. They also reflect what I have heard from colleagues in casual conversations over the years about psychotherapy being largely related to loss—regardless of whether the client's complaint is generalized anxiety that began as persistent worry about loss, depression that developed after numerous losses went unmourned, or phobia that first appeared in loss's fear-filled passageways.

People who are struggling with unresolved grief often don't even know it. They might know something is wrong, that they are struggling, but most of them probably do not go to see psychologists. They may go to physicians because of high blood pressure, ulcers, hives, or some other somatic manifestation of suppressed grief. Or they suffer in private, finding temporary comfort in alcohol or food.

Last year I got a call from a man I had met while serving as a mediator during his contentious divorce ten years previously. Ralph, a hard-driving businessman, was the classic type-A personality. He started a pizza business when he was in college, then sold it to a fraternity brother upon graduation. He took those modest profits and invested them in another business. Over the years, he kept starting, building, and selling businesses, parlaying profits into new ventures with such skill that he soon controlled a complicated and diverse enterprise worth millions. He was always listed among the "rising business stars" in newspaper articles. He had a position of leadership among the other young rising stars of the business community. He was well known and well regarded in the community, both for his business acumen and his philanthropic activities.

He worked all the time. He loved the challenges of his job. He was happiest juggling risks and opportunities, negotiating, and wheeling and dealing. He always said he was doing it for his family but, in truth, could admit he had subordinated most parts of his life to his career. His marriage died of neglect, and he rarely saw his children. He had few friends, all of whom were people from work, and he seemed quite comfortable for it to be that way.

Ralph had first ended up in my office only at the insistence of a Family Division judge who was hearing his divorce petition. We eventually did develop an effective and cordial relationship, but he really had little interest in or use for the psychological dimension of life. After we had accomplished the court-mandated objective of facilitating some communication and decisionmaking between him and his wife, he and I said good-bye not expecting to see one another again.

I was surprised to hear from Ralph again. I was even more surprised when he entered my office. His once-ruddy complexion was sallow. The high-energy self-confidence he formerly radiated was gone. His speech was slow and tentative, he avoided my eyes, and his handshake was limp. He certainly didn't resemble the business leader he had worked so hard to become. Instead, he looked like a beaten man.

"I think I'm having a breakdown," he began, without even pausing for the few brief preliminary pleasantries that ordinarily characterize a person's reappearance after a long absence. He told me that about a year before that, he had gotten a cold that progressed to flu. Since that time, he had been continuously sick, one stomach thing after the other, lots of head colds, infections that would not respond readily to antibiotics. Robust all his life, it seemed strange for him to be so sickly. He went to his doctor, who checked him out thoroughly and ruled him to be in generally good health.

"About two months ago," he continued, the words now spilling out of him as though he couldn't be rid of them fast enough,

> I started becoming exhausted. It got hard for me to make it all the way through a day. I started losing weight and I'm having trouble sleeping. When I do sleep, I have frightening dreams I can't remember when I wake up. My mood is in the dumper. I cry for no reason. Worst of all, I'm so damn lonely I can hardly stand it. I'll be in a meeting, and someone will be talking about some little family business we're looking at buying, and I'll have to excuse myself. I never cried before, and I'm crying all the time, now.

He told me that his family physician eventually prescribed Prozac for depression. "But I couldn't tolerate the side effects. He tried me on some other medicines, but I couldn't stand the way they made me feel, either. I'm getting scared. I think I'm going out of my mind."

His voice cracked. He looked around the room, swallowing hard, his eyes filled with tears. "My doctor thinks this is all in my head. He calls it a mood disorder, so I thought I'd come see you." He turned to face me for the first time since he came in and gave me an embarrassed smile. "You do work with head cases, right?"

At some point in our conversation, I asked him if he could come up with an image describing how he felt during his periods of deepest loneliness and most intense crying. In psychotherapy, it is often helpful to give form and dimension to a person's distress in order to have something to work with, something to change. Sometimes I ask people to draw a picture or name a song, but Ralph was a talker, so I asked him to tell me a story. "Complete this sentence," I said. "When I cry, I feel like . . . ."

Ralph looked up, a hint of his old confident self peeking out from behind his puffy eyelids, and said, "I feel like someone died."

I nodded, pausing a bit to let this characterization sink in for both of us. Then I asked, "Did someone die?"

He closed his eyes, a deflated balloon of a man in an expensive suit, and just sat like that, slumped in the chair, probably unaware that his head was nodding: "Yes." He almost wasn't breathing. Then, eyes still closed, he sighed and began to tell me that what came to his mind when I asked that question was his mother, who had died six years previously.

"It's funny," he added. "I was really close to my mom. I was really upset when she was dying. And I've hardly thought about her since her funeral."

Ralph proceeded to talk about his mother's final pain-filled weeks and his frustration at being helpless to even make her more comfortable. Ralph is practical, used to being in charge. Ralph knows how to make things happen. And how to decide, if there's nothing to be done, to cut losses and move on. It seemed like a waste of time back then for him to dwell on his mother's death after it was over. There was nothing he could do about it. So he cut his losses and moved on.

Ralph believed that there was no point to feeling bad about his mother's death if there was nothing he could do about it. He was mistaken. The very reason we feel bad after someone we love dies is that there is nothing we can do about it.

"It's like I just discarded her," he said, "put her out of my mind after she died."

"Out of your mind?" I asked, echoing his worry about where he was going.

"Yeah, I put her out, like the trash," he answered.

"In the dumper?" I asked, echoing his statement about where his mood had gone.

"That's right," he said.

"That's right," I said. "That is where you stuck her, and it appears to be where you're stuck now." He lowered his face into his hands and began to sob.

I assured Ralph that he was not going out of his mind. Nor did he have a "mood disorder." We're supposed to feel like someone died when someone has, in fact, died. That's mood working as it should.

Moods and emotions tend to respond to what's going on around us and within us. If people feel very sad or very happy, very good or very bad about themselves, or very optimistic or very pessimistic and these feelings do not relate to anything happening around or within them, then mood is out of whack. Arbitrary, random moods not connected to any external reality, which are sufficiently intense or constant to interfere with a person's capacity to function in life, are considered a disorder.

Not feeling like somebody died when somebody died is a mood disorder. Grief only causes a disorder when, like Ralph, we try to get around it and get lost in the detour.

And that is what so many of us do. We run away from grief, or at least we try to. Why? Why do so many of us get stuck in this morass of unfinished good-byes? Is it because we get frightened by the apparent danger and insecurity of our deepest and least tolerable vulnerabilities—our weakness, madness, dependency, and lack of control?

Or is it that grief—that universal and natural function rooted deep within us by which we regain equilibrium after profound loss—just feels so strange, like we are getting sick or losing our minds. Do we balk because, with the decline in the importance of religious and social rituals, we no longer have ceremonies to guide us, as they guided our ancestors, into and through grief's convoluted passages?

Grief is not an illness, but it sure comes on like one. It can disrupt sleep patterns, appetite, capacity for pleasure, and energy levels. Our metabolism rates may change, causing weight loss as rapid as if we had a high fever. One woman told me that she spent days after her mother died vomiting as though she had been poisoned. Another told me she lay awake night after night, eyes wide open, feeling as though she were drunk despite not having had a drink in weeks, her skin hot and gritty as though she had been in the sun too long. A man I know confided that he unexpectedly fell to his knees howling in pain, his arms clasped around his stomach to contain the fiery explosion he felt ripping through him.

Grief hurts. Literally. "Heartsick" is not just a lyrical synonym for sorrow. Neither are "heartache" or "heartbreak." These terms refer to a breath-stopping ache, sometimes located in the chest and sometimes in the pit of the stomach, which can come with loss.

Grief not only makes us feel sick but also makes us feel, and act, kind of crazy. Crazy with fear. Crazy with pain. Crazy with confusion. Crazy by definition: We are temporarily unable to differentiate what's real from what's not real when what's always been completely real completely disappears. I watched one of my friends, ordinarily a trusting and open man, become suspicious, vigilant, and withdrawn after his mother died. I've seen clients become stupid, unable to remember the simplest things, understand or solve the simplest problem. I've seen others start to cry in the middle of a sentence or fly into a rage without warning or provocation.

Grief can make us feel hopeless and helpless. Grief can arouse thoughts of disease and death. It can disrupt our capacity for pleasure, cause difficulty with concentration, and annihilate our self-esteem. All of these can also be characteristics of a mental disorder called depression, but grief is not depression. Grief is not any kind of disorder. Grief is a process during which our minds grapple with and find a way through the tumult of loss.

But it feels like a disorder. It scares us. We try to suppress the impulses it triggers, as we do with anything that poses a threat—and we are well equipped to do so by a lifetime's training in suppressing natural impulses.

Impulse suppression is, after all, what much of our socialization, which begins in childhood and continues throughout our lives, is about. While many species of creatures, like birds or fish, are born with a full array of instincts that equip them with all the skills they'll need to live their lives, we humans must learn to stifle our "natural" ways in order to fit into a family, a tribe, or a society. We learn to restrain many of the spontaneous and automatic responses we have to our needs.

Our basic drive for food, for example, could be quite adequately satisfied by our eating whatever food was handy whenever we were hungry. We would use our hands, grunting our pleasure aloud, occasionally wiping the juices from our chin on our arm and then relieving ourselves with a vigorous belch. As children, however, we are taught to wait until a meal is served, to eat only from the portion on our plate, to manipulate and use culturally mandated utensils, to chew quietly with our mouths closed, to periodically use the napkin resting in our laps to wipe our lips and chin, and to stifle gastric eruptions. We are taught "manners," the ultimate in impulse suppression.

By the time we have become adults, our ability to suppress "natural" ways is well developed. We control our impatience as we wait for the red light to turn green at midnight even though no one is coming the other way. We are able to hold onto an unbearably hot pot if a child is underfoot, even though our involuntary reflex is to jerk our hand away.

We are also able to interrupt our natural grieving, which otherwise might have us howling at the moon or curling up in a ball of pain. We really are too good at suppressing impulses when it comes to grief. We need to grieve if we are to remain healthy.

It's like sleep; imagine that you begin having difficulty keeping your eyes open, start losing coordination, find it difficult to concentrate, get irritable, become unable to communicate. Do these alarming symptoms mean that you are coming down with a terrible disease or that you are losing your mind? Perhaps. But probably, they just mean that you are tired. Should you try fresh air, caffeine, vigorous physical activity, stimulants? Perhaps. But ultimately, the remedy for being tired is to get some sleep.

The remedy for grief is to grieve. And as with sleep, just doing it once won't be enough. Grief's paradox is that trying to resist its summons, for fear it will make us sick, will make us sick.

Suppressed grief may affect our physical well-being, as it had begun to do with Ralph. It can disrupt our psychological well-being, creating discomfort ranging from anxiety to depression. It can also affect how we get along with each other.

Several years ago, Claudia, a single woman in her early thirties, was referred to me by a former client with whom she was in graduate school and to whom she had been complaining about her love life.

She and I met and spoke. She considered the cause of her distress to be her fear of the looming breakup of her current romance. She tearfully told me how tenuous her link with her boyfriend was, how she was always so terrified that he was leaving her, despite his assurances to the contrary. She told me story after story to document her fears, but they were all stories of relatively benign transgressions on his part, incongruent with the intensity of her reaction.

If he was late, it meant that he was out looking to meet another woman and then he was going to dump her. If he forgot to do something, it meant that she was no longer important to him and he was about to dump her. It sounded as if he was a bit inconsiderate at times, perhaps absent-minded at others, but he was never threatening to leave. And she did not impress me as so fragile as to be unable to endure the ordinary give-and-take of romance.

As she began to weave more and more of her past into her narrative, I learned that her second parent had died a month before she met this man. "Meeting George," she said, "saved my life. I don't know how I would have survived losing my mom without him. I don't know where I'd be now if not for him. Probably in an insane asylum. And I'm so afraid of where I'd end up if he left me now. I'm always so afraid he'll leave me if I complain. So I don't complain, but it's driving me crazy."

I pointed out that she appeared to be in a bit of a bind. On the one hand, she couldn't stand being in a relationship in which every action on the man's part became an echo of abandonment she so dreaded. It was making her crazy. On the other hand, she couldn't stand getting out of a relationship that seemed to provide some insulation between herself and her grief over the actual abandonment she experienced when her mother had died. Ending it would reopen that old wound, which she also feared would make her crazy.

I wondered aloud if, perhaps, she would consider temporarily suspending her deliberations about what to do about her love life and turn her attention instead to her parents, following me into the grief for them that seemed to have been suspended when she met George.

"I'm okay about my parents' deaths now," she said. "I cried as much as I think I needed to. I really just need to figure out what to do about George." She thanked me, paid me for the session, and left.

About a year later, her name showed up again on my appointment list. When she arrived, we sat comfortably together, and she brought me up to date. Since our prior meeting, she had finished school, gotten a job, broken off her relationship with George, and fallen madly in love, almost immediately, with a man nicknamed Red, who had, at first, appeared much superior to George in every way. But now the same thing was happening. Red was driving her crazy, just the way George had, by doing little things that scared and annoyed her, about which she was afraid to complain lest he decide to leave her.

She had remembered our earlier conversation. Now she could see the pattern developing: The boyfriends might be insulation, but she was not escaping the storm. She was beginning to suspect that she was unlikely to form a mature relationship until she first got down to finishing grieving for her parents.

Neither Ralph nor Claudia had any idea, at first, what lay at the root of their predicaments. Once they had the information that it was unfinished grief, they had the chance to begin facing their losses, letting themselves be affected by them, and slowly giving in to what had happened in their lives—the only true path out of their plight.

Each of them worked with me for several months, telling me stories about their parents, sharing photographs of their families, crying, laughing, and savoring the richness of the legacy they were left with. Ralph began spending much more time with his children, who were young adults by then but both eagerly welcoming of their dad into their lives. And Claudia started separating her relationship with Red from her relationships with her parents. Her romance became much more serious, and Red never did leave.

Some of us try to slip past grief's turbulence because of a fear that the passage through grief is not survivable—that it will be totally engulfing and will last forever. Perhaps we fear that there is no life for us after the death of a loved one, that our minds and hearts will remain chaotic and pain-filled forever. That we'll never get over it. So we avoid getting into it.

And some of us fear that if we really grieve, we really *will* get over it, and then we will have lost our loved one forever. Perhaps avoiding grief is a way of holding loss at bay.

Few of us, to be sure, walk around after someone we love dies realizing that the grief we feel is good for us.

Misunderstanding grief is not necessarily a result of lacking information. I'm a psychologist. I know a lot about what goes on when people grieve, and when my parents died, I became as entangled as anyone else between my impulses to grieve and my impulses to flee.

It wasn't until months after I buried my mother that I realized that the peculiar ways I was feeling and acting were born of my reluctance to grieve her and my father's deaths. Then I was able to start doing the things I needed to do to profess my grief like visiting their grave, planting a garden in their memory, hanging family pictures on the wall, praying, and making connections with extended far-flung family members.

And I learned, firsthand, that intense grief—whether it manifests itself as sorrow, tears, remembrances, anger, or feelings of helplessness—is not constant and does not last forever. Grief comes in waves that last for a while and then abate. We get distracted for a while by something else—a phone call, hitting our thumb with a hammer, having to park the car in a very tight space. Lonely times are interrupted for a while by visiting friends. Pain and fear-filled thoughts temporarily yield to happy or amusing reminiscences. We feel better and, mistakenly, think grief is over, only to be discouraged by its return with the next wave.

We do not pass through grief in a straight line. We do not start feeling better and then, bit by bit, get better and better, each day an improvement over the day before, each week easier than the one it follows. The recovery from loss is much more erratic than that. It is characterized by times of feeling pretty good, in which we dare to believe that crying time might be almost over, followed by crushing times of feeling much worse, in which we believe crying time will never end.

As grief begins to resolve itself, over time we do begin to notice that we are feeling better. The waves of grief have begun to change. They change in frequency, gradually coming less often. They change in intensity, gradually feeling less profound. And they change in duration, eventually lasting less long.

Bit by bit, storms blow themselves out. Grief subsides. Our voyage can then continue, somewhat more serenely, toward its mysterious destination.

The memories return

"Don't worry,"
Rachel said,
"if your memories
of your mother
disappear.

After a few months
they will be back
fresher that ever."

It's true.
The memories of her last difficult days
have faded.
Two days ago she appeared to me
wearing the green & white striped cotton dress
she had when I was a kid, in the 1940s,
in her forties,
her lovely dark hair
yet to be lovely silver.

Today I wore her string of pearls,
knowing that wearing them against the skin
renews their lustre.

—Karen Ethelsdattar
Jersey City, NJ

8

Learning to Swim

Techniques of Grief

"Go ahead, tell him what you were telling me," the dental hygienist said to me when the young dentist, new to the practice I've been going to for years, entered the room.

With his crisp white jacket and military brush-cut hair, he was the picture of brisk professionalism. He snapped on his gloves, preparing for the examination.

"Go on," she prompted me. "Tell him about your book. He really needs to know. His father died last month, and he's been a complete mess."

The now-puzzled dentist turned and asked, "My father?"

"He's writing a book about what happens when parents die," she said.

The dentist slowly lowered himself onto the stool next to my chair and slid it over to where I could see him. "Really?" he asked, softly. He appeared to be wilting.

"Then maybe you can tell me," he continued, "how do I get through this?"

For many of us, this really is the only important question. How *are* we to get through the surreal time that so often follows the death of parents? How are we to navigate, being so disoriented, through all that agitation, pain, sadness, regret, and heady liberation that floods our bodies, minds, and spirits? Just how do we get through this thing called grief?

As a psychologist, I am often in a position to talk with people in the grip of transforming life crises. However, being nearly supine in a dentist's chair with a blue paper napkin clipped to my shirt-front, I was not in a position in which I felt comfortable dispensing advice.

"Well, for starters," I said, "I'd recommend that you be careful to keep breathing."

This might sound flip, but it wasn't. There really are techniques to help us get through the frightening and tangled challenge of loss—ways to manage runaway thoughts, embrace unfamiliar emotions, and find the support we need—that are as basic as breathing.

Learning to grieve is a lot like learning to swim. I remember looking around the pool as a little boy, seeing all those swimmers and wishing that I could be one, too. But I did not even know how to float. I couldn't imagine putting my face in the water, lying down, and not sinking. Each time I tried, I would begin thrashing, choke on the water, and become even more frightened.

Eventually, I succeeded. Not by trying harder or thrashing harder. When I finally made it happen, I had stopped trying to make it happen. What we really learn when we learn to float is, well, that we float. As long as we think there is something else to it, something we do not yet know, we remain too afraid to let go of the side of the pool.

In grief, as in a swimming pool, the way to do it is by letting it happen.

Keep It Small and Simple

In an attempt to get some handle on the strangeness of the grief experience, many of us make the mistake of trying to predict its course. We want to know how to get through grief, how much time it will take. Despite having no idea what lies ahead, we start doing what we think of as making a plan.

"I feel terrible right now," we think, "and I know I'm going to feel terrible tomorrow." Then, we scare ourselves: "What if I still feel terrible next week? Next month? There's that woman I heard about who still feels terrible, and it's been years since her mother died." Soon, we are aloft, in full-panicked mental flight, on the broken wings of despair disguised as thoughtful fore-sight.

We are not analyzing our situation or planning or thinking at these times. We are trying to rush ourselves through an incom-prehensible and thoroughly unpleasant experience, endeavoring to make it be over faster by pretending ourselves into the future. Understandable though this is, all we actually accomplish is to scare ourselves. Despite the greatness of our imaginations, we cannot get to the future before it arrives.

Imagine all the meals you will ever eat and then try to con-sume them in one swallow. Impossible! Imagine all the stairs you will climb this year, then try to take them all right now. Exhausting! Imagine all the chores you'll do next week, but just try getting them done before supper. Hopeless!

Such imagining is meaningless. Meals have to be eaten a bite at a time. Only one step can be taken, and then we take the next one. Chores get done as we get to them.

Grief must be traversed moment by moment.

When I am working with people who are scaring themselves in this way, I recommend that they keep their imagination in check by setting very limited goals relative to time. For example, a thought like "getting through the rest of my life without mother" is way too big and will certainly trigger one of these terrifying episodes. "Getting through the rest of today" might even be too much. Get focused on getting through a much smaller period of time, instead, and stop the panic. Can you imagine getting through another hour? If that feels too daunting, how about a half hour? Fifteen minutes? A minute? A few seconds? Most of us can get through a few seconds of just about anything. And anyway, you have to get through the next few seconds before getting on to "the rest of your life."

After you get through the next few seconds, then just get through the next few seconds.

Keep it small and simple.

Trying to figure out how to accomplish all there is to get done after parents die is another way that we inadvertently overwhelm ourselves. We might start out thinking about making some necessary arrangement, such as "I have to call the funeral director." But then our thoughts take off: "And then I have to notify the lawyer, and then the minister, and then I have to go through their things, and then I have to sell their house, and then there's the holidays and how will I get through them—and then—" And then, once again, we are aloft on the wings of fear.

I recommend picking one small task and seeing if it is possible to focus on just that. For instance, see if you can focus on just calling the funeral director. If that starts skidding out of control, make the task smaller. How about merely dialing the phone number? Could you focus on just doing that without any other thoughts or worries intruding? If even that starts getting too big, how about just one digit of the number? Can you focus on doing just that? Just picking up the phone? Reaching for the phone? Walking over to the phone?

It really doesn't matter how it's organized in our thoughts. The point is that we have to control our thoughts in order to be able to gradually move from one moment to the next. We can do this only by shortening our gaze and paying attention to the moment we are in. If we get ahead of ourselves, simultaneously thinking about the next moment and the moment beyond that, we stop being able to move altogether.

Health

The bereft are exhausted. Emotions activated by grief—sorrow, anger, fear, remorse, and so on—require a lot of energy. Expressing emotions, whether by crying, raging, or sulking, uses energy. Suppressing emotions to conceal them from ourselves and others uses even more energy. Becoming increasingly vigilant in response to strange circumstances uses energy. Struggling to understand and solve problems with which we are unaccustomed, especially when resources are already depleted, uses energy.

Grief is hard work.

Our primitive ancestors were built for hard work. Every day they were challenged to catch dinner and escape predators. Their bodies evolved the capacity of becoming very efficient, accustomed to very quickly and briefly diverting energy from complex systems (e.g., the digestive and the immune systems) to more primitive ones (e.g., the long muscles and cardiovascular systems) when they needed power and stamina to run fast or fight hard.

In modern times, we neither have to chase our food or avoid becoming dinner. Instead, we are challenged by stressors, like the emotions of grief, which, although hard work, are psychological in nature and therefore last much longer than the few minutes of a hunt or a chase. Even though they are no longer adaptive, our primitive emergency mechanisms still take over when we are performing this type of hard work: Our bodies still become more efficient; energy still gets diverted from more complex systems to more primitive ones; and the immune system, one of our most complex, is suppressed.

With immune functions compromised, we become extrasusceptible to contagious illnesses carried by other people, as well as to the viruses and dormant diseases lurking within our bodies. That's why people often get sick in prolonged periods of high stress.

In fact, getting sick is one of the most probable complications of grief. Taking extra care to stay healthy is paramount. In particular, I advise people to pay attention to nutrition, especially during the first months after a loss, because appetite, the natural motivation for balanced eating, is typically impaired. Those hungers we do experience are for foods that are comforting rather than nutritious, like fats and sweets.

I recommend at least one wholesome meal every day, even if it is only soup. In addition, I recommend taking a daily multivitamin, being monitored by the family physician and dentist (the chemical balance in the mouth may change, adversely affecting teeth and gums), and getting some exercise on a daily basis.

"Whoa!" some people have said. "You want me to make sure I eat a balanced diet, take vitamins, call my doctor and my dentist, and work out? Oh, please! It's all I can do to get to the couch with my bag of potato chips and figure out which channel my soap opera is on."

Remember the guiding principle: Keep it small and simple. If all you can do is pop a vitamin pill on your way to the couch, good enough. If you can munch on a carrot along with those potato chips, that would be good, too. And when you feel up to it, take a short walk. It'll be good for you, and it will help offset the feeling of helplessness so prevalent in grief's earliest stages.

And then there's breathing. Making sure to breathe deliberately, carefully, and regularly is an example of something small and simple that is both crucial and immediately beneficial. But breathing seems so elementary. You inhale, then you exhale. What's the big deal?

When we are distressed, most of us start breathing erratically without realizing it. Sometimes we hold our breath. We actually stop breathing for periods of ten, fifteen, or twenty seconds at a time, creating a state of mild oxygen deprivation similar to suffocation. At other times, we begin a pattern of rapid and shallow breathing that creates a hyperventilated state, producing light-headedness and nervousness. Whether we hold our breath or pant, our thinking becomes clouded, and we become more frightened.

When I am working with a client who is having difficulty breathing, I recommend a method I learned from a Yoga instructor years ago:

Place your hands on your abdomen in such a manner that your fingers are resting on your belly just below your belt line. Now imagine that a string is attached to your body slightly below your navel. When you want to inhale, pull on the loose end of the string. Let it go when you want to exhale. Breathe like that for the next few minutes, pulling the string when you feel the need to inhale and letting it go to exhale. Pull, inhale. Release, exhale. In. Out. In. Out.

Experiment by pulling the string farther out and notice how much more deeply you are able to inhale. Gradually become aware that your fingers, still resting on your lower abdomen, are being moved by your breathing. They move each time you inhale because your belly swells and lifts them. They move each time you exhale as your belly settles. As you swell and settle, and your fingers move up and down, your chest will remain relatively still. Feel your abdomen press against your belt each time it expands. Feel it sink each time you exhale. This is diaphragmatic breathing, or breathing from the diaphragm. This is how to breathe carefully and regularly, ensuring that you will neither be hyperventilating nor suffocating.

Perhaps one afternoon, as you sit on that sofa watching soap operas, you will remember to place your fingers on your abdomen and check whether you are breathing deeply and satis-fyingly from your diaphragm. Each time you do just that one small and simple thing, you will be taking a big step toward tak-ing good care of yourself.

Support

Nobody gets through grief alone. The expectation that we be able to single-handedly traverse the unfamiliar and frightening terrain of parental death, or any other loss for that matter, has no more basis than that we should be able to fly to the moon without knowing how to operate a rocket. Like any other journey into the dark, what most of us need when we grieve is a combination of reassurance, information, and support. We need to know that the crossing upon which we are embarking is survivable. We need some guidance from those who know a bit about it. And we need the support and affection of those who love us.

We need other people because we need to be reminded that we are connected to humanity when fundamental attachments are severed by death. We need to borrow courage from other people—to be "en-couraged" by them—when we become afraid. We need help from other people because grief is just too big for most of us to get through alone.

There are so many ways people can provide relief—if they know you need it. Ask a friend to come along and sit with you while you do an unpleasant task like going through your par-ents' closets. Ask a neighbor to watch your children for an after-noon so you can have some relief. Ask the group at church to prepare a meal and spare you that responsibility for a day. Ask a colleague to go for a walk with you at lunchtime to get you away from your telephone. Ask a friend who has been parentless for a while to talk to you about what was helpful, what got in the way.

Ask. Ask. Ask.

Ask someone to help you with decisions. Most of us are completely unfamiliar with the kinds of decisions we are called upon to make after parents die, from buying cemetery plots to going through parents' personal papers. This is a terrible time for solving problems and making decisions. Our judgment and problem-solving skills are completely compromised. Ask a friend to help.

Almost everything that comes up can be postponed without consequence. How to dispose of parents' things, what to do with inherited money, and getting back to work do not present the urgency that they seem to. Put off all you can. Make as few decisions as possible for as long as possible. Remember, keep it small and simple.

Others may insist that you make decisions. Tell them to wait. It is not at all uncommon for heirs to close up parental homes for a year or longer until they feel more able to confront the contents. Park the parents' car somewhere until its disposition can be calmly decided. Deposit inherited money in a savings account, where it will be safe, until you feel ready to make other choices.

Engage a trustworthy and disinterested third party to assist, whether it be to review and sign legal papers, empty an apartment and locate temporary storage facilities, inventory a bank safety-deposit box, notify social security and life insurance agencies, pay parental bills, cancel appointments made long ago, or terminate unnecessary services.

Call the family lawyer. If you do not know a lawyer, ask for recommendations from friends. Consult with your clergy. Call the funeral director, often a very knowledgeable and underappreciated professional who can be extremely helpful at these times. Get help. Don't try to do this alone.

Someone else's judgment and oversight can also be a priceless form of protection against opportunists who are drawn to personal tragedy the way rats are drawn to spilled corn.

Occasionally, people will disappoint you. Even those who are generous by nature and want to help may just not know how to be helpful, and you may find their well-intentioned but clumsy attempts upsetting. Forgive them, and look for help elsewhere. Keep it simple.

Some may not know what to say when expressing condolences. They might say, "I know how bad you must be feeling." They might say, "They were so old and so sick for so long. This must be a great relief for you." They might even say, "Oh, my," with surprise that sounds like disapproval, "you're still feeling so bad even after all these weeks?"

How can you respond to such awkward moments? I found that by replying with two stock answers—"Yes, that's right. Thank you." or "Yes, this has been difficult."—spared me from having to plumb my already depleted resources for a new answer each time. And, possibly even more important, I was spared the embarrassment of unloading my mournful wrath on someone whose only transgression was that they lacked skills in expressing sympathy. It is much simpler to forgive them.

If your personal world does not contain enough understanding friends or if you are uncomfortable burdening people you know with your troubles, join a grief support or recovery group. Some types are peer operated, others are facilitated by professionals—either will be composed of warm, caring people, often in pain themselves, who can provide support and information. Many offer anonymity, which may be helpful in expressing the more unattractive or shameful aspects of grief. More important, they provide an opportunity to share the burden.

Support groups advertise in local papers, in city magazines, and on the Internet. If you cannot easily find one in your community, ask your physician, attorney, hospital, or hospice social worker, member of the clergy, or funeral director. Call the United Way, Visiting Nurses Association, community mental health center, or the local chapter of the American Red Cross. Someone will know where these groups meet and how to contact them. Ask.

It may be helpful to go to a professional counselor in times of grief. Mental health specialists proficient in working with grief come from many backgrounds: religion, social work, psychology, psychiatry, nursing. Talking with a professional offers an opportunity to put concerns into words and explore what it feels like to say them and what it sounds like to hear them. For instance, someone might say, "My husband has been no help at all throughout this entire time," listen to the words as they are saying them, and realize that the judgment is either inaccurate or much too harsh.

Saying private thoughts aloud to another person helps us gain perspective and evaluate our situation. Saying "My husband has been no help at all" to a friend or another family member, however, can create hard feelings toward the husband, complicating rather than clarifying the situation.

That's where a therapist can be helpful. The therapist doesn't know the husband, has no personal stake in the marriage, and won't take sides. Therapists know how to listen with interest while people talk. And they often ask helpful questions.

A relationship with a therapist is very clearly defined and agreed to in advance. Therapists do not expect those who seek their assistance to, in turn, listen to their problems. They do not expect unspecified future favors in exchange for the attention they provide. A therapist provides a safe place to talk and listens with interest and respect.

A lot of times, mourners really believe they are going crazy. A therapist may be able to confirm or rule this out. Some mourners really do require the temporary use of medication to expedite their grief. For others, medication would just cause a delay. Therapists have diagnostic tests and standardized methods of interviewing that can differentiate between perilous and merely acute grief. They can offer informed guidance.

But remember, all professionals are not the same. The less experienced with grief a therapist is, the more likely it is that this therapist may be alarmed by grief's more passionate manifestations. Be sure to select a counselor who has both personal experience and professional background with grief.

Your first question to a therapist should be: "Have you lost your parents or any loved ones?" Find someone who has been through it.

So go see a counselor, join a support group, get assistance from an attorney or funeral director, reach out to neighbors and friends. We need help to get through grief in so many ways. And in many instances, people really want to be helpful. Offer to be generous with your needs and fears. Give other people the opportunity, and the pleasure, of helping.

Memorials

Somebody recently told me that she had scattered her parents' ashes at sea, as stipulated in their will, and then wished she had kept back enough of their remains to bury near her house. "I have nowhere to visit," she said, "nowhere to go when I want to sit quietly and remember them."

I have found that having a cemetery plot and a headstone engraved with their name has been helpful to me when I need a place to go, sit, and think about my parents. Many of the people I have spoken to over the years have agreed that they feel comforted by some tangible representation of their deceased loved ones.

Memorials are, of course, not limited to graves. Once a man took me to see the flower garden he had planted in his parents' memory, where he toils every weekend from late winter to late fall. He told me that he feels close to them again whenever he works there. I know a woman who bought a large sofa that, for some reason, reminded her of her parents. She enjoys sitting on it at the end of a busy workday. Another told me she had hung a landscape her father had painted in a prominent place of honor in her home, and it seems to watch out for her. One man even told me that he had thrown a subway token from his father's change purse out of his car window on his way to work, and now he thinks of his father every time he passes that spot.

I had a friend, Lenny, who lost his father suddenly and violently in an airline disaster. He was unable to find peace. Since the body had never been recovered, there was nothing to bury. There was no grave to visit. Although a memorial plaque was placed near the site of the accident, Lenny had no connection to it. He wanted to create a spot, at least in his mind, where he could go for his memories of his father in happier times. He felt stumped.

I invited Lenny to come with me to a memorial grove that we maintain on our farm. My wife and I named our farm "Sweetwater" because of the abundance of sugar maple trees on the property, "sweet water" being the name farmers give to sugar maple sap. I remember telling Lenny that I like to think of those drops of sap, that "sweet water," as the tears of those trees.

Lenny came out to the grove, and we sat together for several hours, looking at the trees. He talked about his father. He told me stories about their going fishing together when he was a youngster, how both of them enjoyed being outdoors. He laughed about the Halloween pranks his family had been playing on each other for as long as he could remember. He talked about how good his father had been with his mother while she was dying, and he cried when he remembered the terrible day he was called by the airline representative about the accident.

We walked over to some saplings. Lenny selected a healthy five-footer. We dug up, put it in a wheelbarrow, and carted it out to a clearing he had chosen. He dug the hole, and together, we wrestled the ball into the ground and covered it with dirt.

Afterward, we stood together for a few minutes, our heads bowed. Lenny told me how wonderful it was for him to know that this tree, planted in his father's memory, would awaken each year from its annual winter slumber and weep.

Anyone can plant a tree. Or get a stone from a favorite childhood vacation spot, or find something personal among parents' things and put it somewhere in the house or in the yard, or, for that matter, in the mind, where it can serve as a tribute. Such commemoration is not morbid. Quite the opposite. It can be very comforting. And to the extent that it helps the mourner adapt to the new and complicated fact of parental deaths as well as heal the pains of grief, it is life enhancing and reaffirming.

Memorials can even be created from stories, from oral histories. Mourners, by nature, seem compelled to share stories about the deceased. Family members and close friends, sitting together after a funeral or during the months that follow, spontaneously begin swapping anecdotes and comparing accounts of times they shared with the departed. These tales are simultaneously each person's claims on a connection to the missing and missed, as well as an admission ticket to membership among the forsaken.

It doesn't usually take much to set off one of these impromptu reminiscent exchanges. Old scrapbooks and photo albums are full of stories to share. Finding some old family souvenir will certainly encourage someone. Listening to old recordings of favorite music conjures up memories. Sitting together and watching old home movies, we can remember our parents as vital young adults and ourselves as children.

But here, too, remember to keep it small and simple. There is no need to chronicle the entire family history in a documentary or to publish a web site in memory of your mother. A set of chipped tea cups, a leaf pressed between two books that falls to the floor when bookshelves are dismantled—anything can trigger a flood of memory. A pipe rack, a half-empty bottle of cologne, that screwdriver with the loose handle—these are not just things, they are links to a shared past.

Gradually, with unconscious cooperation, survivors weave a commemorative tapestry from these bits and pieces of shared nostalgia. An anecdote here, a disappointment there, hilarity, embarrassment, hurt feelings, warm sentiments. Story by story, smile by smile, and tear by tear, these memories intertwine, creating a fabric in which an image of the departed is preserved, within which survivors are enveloped, and by which they are forever bound.

Get a Break

Grief is tiring. Emotions wrung out, bodies exhausted, spirits overburdened—the bereft are exhausted. And then there's grief's crony, insomnia.

Lack of sleep has a cumulative effect. Its victims start dreading bedtime, knowing each evening that come nightfall, they will probably lie there, yet again, their eyes open, their thoughts racing. Getting some sleep, or at least some rest, becomes a preoccupation, eventually crowding out virtually all other desires.

Turning to alcohol for relief at such times is a bad idea for a number of reasons, chief among which is that it doesn't help. Alcohol has sedating qualities, so we may feel somewhat calmer shortly after a drink or two. However, alcohol has the effect of suppressing energy and, more significantly, subduing mood. The last thing mourners, already out of gas and downhearted, need is an even lower energy level and darker mood—to say nothing of the risk of alcohol-related dependency and disease.

Take time for rest, recreation, distraction, and restoration. Not just sleep or nap-related rest, either. Just as the body requires nutrition for health, the spirit yearns to be fed. Get a break, but remember to keep it small and simple. Find out what inspires and restores you, then go do it. Take in a movie, watch television, or have dinner with friends at a restaurant. Read some poetry you love, listen to music, or take walks in beautiful places. Let yourself be soothed by soaking in a warm relaxing bath. Be invigorated by going dancing. Go bowling. Go to church. Take a drive in the country. Get some ice cream. Get a massage or a manicure, or both. Get on a highway, open all the windows, and sing as loud as you can. Any enjoyable or amusing diversion provides fuel for an aching, exhausted heart.

Perhaps, however, the most important break, the one that only you can provide, is to release yourself from any expectation that you get through this chaotic time with any grace. Expect to be clumsy. Expect to be undignified. Each of us must find out how we grieve, and just about all of us do it in an ungainly fashion. No one has ever told me that they looked back on a period of grief regretting that their performance was not preserved on film. Some of us not only cry, we wail. Some feel angry all the time and snap at strangers. Others get all dressed up in outlandish outfits, while others refuse to bathe for days. The ordinary expressions of grief cover a range of conduct so wide as to be virtually inclusive of every unattractive and undesirable trait imaginable.

Grief cannot be done skillfully, artfully, or beautifully. The bereft earn no points for style or difficulty; there is no concluding moment to grief, arms raised in triumph like an Olympic athlete awaiting a score.

The goal of grief is neither achievement nor excellence. The goal is to get through it.

Prayer

When people ask for guidance to get through times of great sorrow, I usually include the recommendation that they pray. If they ask me how, I reply, "However you pray will be fine."

If they say they are nonbelievers, I tell them that belief is not required in order for prayer to be helpful.

If they say they do not know how to pray, I tell them, "Well, then, that'll be the first thing you can pray for."

Just about everybody prays, one way or another. Some people kneel in a pew and recite venerable litanies, whereas others merely pause before meals or bedtime. I know some who fold their hands and assume a position of supplication while they express gratitude and humility, others who seek grace or make requests for themselves and their loved ones. Some pray in cathedrals, churches, or synagogues. Others at Buddhist chants or at Friends meetings. I know people who hike into the woods or go to the ocean and become lost in nature's majesty.

I know lots more who never enter any religious building, be it church, mosque, synagogue, or meetinghouse. They claim no religious affiliation, no faith of any kind. But they cry out indignantly at the injustices life throws their way. I wonder to whom they are speaking.

I do not encourage people to pray in order to convert them to a particular religion or, for that matter, to religion at all. The ways in which someone perceives the mysteries of the universe, understands life's meaning, or wrestles with good and evil are personal. They are certainly not my business—literally. If someone asks for guidance in such matters, I refer them to the specialists: the clergy.

I encourage people to pray, by themselves or in prayer groups, for one reason—I see that it works. Prayer causes something unexpectedly restorative and wonderful to happen in healing people's hearts. Prayer is good for us. Prayer helps us to recover faster and to live our lives more fully.

I'm not referring to prayer in the "crutches dropping and walking by himself for the first time, praise Jesus" tradition of faith healers. Although their work may be very helpful to the devout, that's not what I mean. Rather, I simply mean that over the years I have observed that people who have come to me for help who also pray—regardless of their religious affiliation, what they hold sacred, or how dogmatically they observe the doctrines of their faith—seem to get their lives going in satisfying ways and start feeling whole again faster than those who do not pray.

I encourage people to pray because I have observed a direct connection between prayer and recovery.

I cannot say why this happens. But then, come to think of it, I have no idea how a television works either. I just know which buttons to push. I don't understand how flowers grow. I just weed, fertilize, and water. The flower takes care of the rest.

I don't know how or why prayer helps. I have just seen that it does.

A growing body of scientific research seems to be coming to the same conclusion. Within the past twenty years, articles in juried medical journals are increasingly reporting an association between greater religious involvement and lower blood pressure, fewer strokes, lower death rates from heart disease, lower mortality and faster recovery after heart surgery, longer lives, and better general health.

So I encourage people to pray. But some tell me that they just can't. They tell me they find it too difficult, too embarrassing, or even repugnant. They say they are too angry or too full of doubt.

"In that case," I tell them, "ask any of your friends or family who do pray to include you in their prayers." I tell them this because I've seen "intercessory prayer"—one person praying for another—work, too.

Scientific studies support this observation, as well. Probably the best known was conducted in 1988 by Randolph Byrd, a cardiologist at the University of California at San Francisco. Dr. Byrd arranged for nearly 400 heart attack patients to be randomly divided into two groups. All the patients got identical standard medical care. The only difference was that volunteers were asked to pray for the recovery of members of one group. Dr. Byrd was the only person in contact with patients who knew a study was being conducted, and he did not know who was assigned to which group.

The outcome for the two groups was dramatically different: Patients in the group for which prayers were said required fewer antibiotics, suffered less subsequent congestive heart failure, and had a lower incidence of pneumonia.

Prayer really does cause something unexpectedly restorative and wonderful to happen in healing people's hearts.

Trust

Getting through a time as painful and demanding as mourning requires that we trust in life's renewable and sustainable potential. We must have confidence that "this, too, shall pass." But at first, we don't. Grief feels like the beginning of some dark new forever. It feels impossible to survive intact, much less come out the other side.

"I'm really afraid that I'm going to feel this way from now on," people say to me. "I've never felt so awful. I never even imagined I could feel so awful."

Fear is not a source of good predictions. For that matter, there is only one good prediction: Everything changes. That's the realization that scares us when somebody we love dies in the first place. Why not use the same realization when it comes to reassuring us that the pain of loss will pass, too?

Whether we are aware of it or not, getting through life in its most ordinary times takes a lot of trust. Why don't we panic at night when the sun goes down and the world becomes dark? After all, we don't think, "Oh, no! The light is going away and darkness shall forever now prevail!" Instead, we trust that the sun will rise the next morning and the light will return.

Why don't we collapse in terror that the earth is dying every winter when plants shrivel, the nights get long, and the air gets cold? Again, we don't think, "Oh, no! All life is at an end!"—because we trust that spring will appear in a few months and vitality will return to the land.

We do not become afraid when we descend into that darkness because we are familiar with the cycles of the sun and the seasons. But we are not familiar with the rhythms of grief, so it's hard to trust.

"I need a sign," a client once demanded.

Fortunately, recovery from grief provides one. "It'll come to you some morning after you have been awake for about a minute or so," I told her. "Suddenly you'll start feeling lousy. And then you'll realize that you had been awake for a minute or so before feeling lousy."

That's the sign: for the first time, not waking up already clenched in grief's oppressive embrace. It takes a minute or so to remember our misery.

For most of us, this first glimpse of freedom is when we know that grief will end. We awaken and, ever so briefly, feel normal. We start thinking about what waking people think about—an aching back, the carpool schedule, or the program on the clock radio. We awaken, and amazingly, we are not grieving. That's the sign that foreshadows grief's ebb and the time of rebuilding. It promises that we shall survive, that "this, too, shall pass."

That's when we realize that it is safe to trust again.

For me, it was a moment reminiscent of the first time I actually floated in water and realized that it happened because I had stopped trying to make it happen. It was like the first time it was safe for me to let go of the side of the pool.

Until that morning, keep it small and simple. If you need to struggle with something big and incomprehensible, ponder the sun, the moon, and the millions of stars that nightly arrive and depart, and then next night arrive again, in a tempo as familiar as the rise and fall of our own abdomens as we inhale and exhale. Reliable, trustworthy enigmas, they are as unknowable as the secrets that wound and heal our breakable and infinitely renewable hearts.

The Oval Frame

My mother stands in an oval frame
that crops the top of her hair, the tips
of her toes. She holds one arm in front
at her waist, one arm behind,
posing like a model beside our house
in an oil camp in Venezuela.
The veins on her hand stand out as mine do.
She is only two years older than I am now.
I recognized her square jaw on my face
the year she died, but today I cover
the top half of her face and I know the smile,
the teeth are mine and the eyes squinting
in the sun, the thin arms, the small
bust, the wide hips. At her funeral,
three years ago, someone said, "You look
just like your mother," and I smiled politely.
Now every year that takes me further from her life,
brings me closer to her face, her laugh,
the person I have become, the person
I am yet to be.

—**Pamela Portwood**
Tucson, AZ

The Lesson

*What We Can Learn
from Parental Death*

Life provides each of us with ongoing opportunities for learning, but the instruction is never free. Typically, the more valuable the lesson, the higher the price.

Parental death is a required course. Everyone is enrolled. Everyone pays tuition in the form of grief. Nearly everyone learns something valuable.

There are some exceptions, rare instances in which parental death is an event of little emotional significance, from which its survivors learn little. According to a 1982 study from the University of Minnesota, parental death may be something of a nonevent when the death has been anticipated for a long time and the parent is extremely old, is living in an institution, is no longer fulfilling any parental functions, is emotionally detached from family members, and is the same gender as the survivor.

Death, in such extreme circumstances, is really an anticlimax, more of a blessed release from the protracted and expensive nightmare of parental languishing than the loss of a vitally involved loved one. Typically in such cases, the loss, the grief, and the lesson have occurred previously.

There are also circumstances in which parental death is so catastrophic and its impact on survivors so traumatic that nothing is learned. Instead, the survivors withdraw from life, their worlds dwindle, and their spirits shrivel. For instance, a few of those who lost families in the Holocaust had this reaction.

For the majority of us, however, regardless of the age and health of our parents, where and how they live, their religion, ethnicity, attitude toward death, how we get along with them, or the way in which they die, parental death marks the beginning of an involuntary and distinctively instructive journey.

What can we learn?

Courage

One of the most persistent and inconsolable fears of childhood is that our parents might die, leaving us abandoned. This is one of the reasons bedtime is so frightening for children. Nightly traditions, often devised originally to help children settle down, come to represent unspoken but heartfelt assurances that parents will still be around in the morning. Whether it is a cookie and a bit of juice before bed, reading a book together, saying prayers, or some ritualized exchange of I-love-you's, such recurrent practices of childhood bedtime help ease our primitive terror.

But they do not make it go away. Nothing makes it go away.

The fear of abandonment, particularly abandonment through parental death, remains a source of apprehension throughout our lives. As adults, our fear that parents might die is gradually replaced by the growing, numbing certainty that their death is approaching.

It doesn't seem to matter how old we get, how accomplished we become, how close we are with our parents, how many scary ordeals we have already survived, or how unwavering our religious faith. Fear of parental death continues to loom, and it becomes more threatening as parents age and become more feeble.

This dread, coupled with our culture's inclination to avoid dealing with death altogether, renders most of us uncomfortable in the presence of those who are grieving. Of course, we learn to say the right things: "I'm so sorry" or "My prayers are with you." We even learn to do the right things, such as make contributions to a charity in memory of the deceased, send flowers to the church, or show up at the funeral and hug the mourners.

But most of us feel awkward with the bereft. We remain reserved. We stand back a bit. We maintain a distance between ourselves and the grief of the survivors, understanding the loss as *theirs*. Our role is to be *there* for *them*.

My personal introduction to death occurred when I returned to college for my sophomore year and learned that my friend, Mace, had died over the summer while on a trip to Mexico. I had wonderful memories of times with this bright, funny, and athletic young man, and I knew I would miss him.

At virtually the same time, however, I also learned that some other friends from the previous year would not be returning to school: Some had transferred, some had dropped out to enlist in the military, and one had decided to stay in Europe to "find himself."

I wrote a note of condolence to Mace's family and looked up his former roommate to commiserate. I remember being struck by how strange it seemed that Mace, so vital at the end of school the previous summer, could get sick and die in only a few short months.

But I defended myself from feeling the full impact of *my* loss by rationalizing. I gave Mace's premature death the same personal meaning I gave to my other friends' not coming back to school—I wouldn't be seeing him again.

His death belonged to his parents and the rest of his family, not to me. I remained behind a shield.

That was pretty much how it was for me every time death intruded on my fragile and innocent sense of safety. I would attend the funeral when someone I knew died. I would feel, and express, genuine sympathy to their families. I would even steel myself to go up and view the remains when the casket was open during funeral home visitation. But I felt apprehensive, uncomfortable, and I kept the experience at arm's length. I minimized the confusion, fear, and especially the echo of that childhood terror of losing parents, by justifying the loss as not really mine.

I was willing to be *there* (some place other than where I was) for *them* (people other than me), and I felt generous being so accommodating.

Even when my father died, I was able to dilute the experience somewhat by diverting my attention to my mother, even though she was already in a rather advanced stage of dementia and may not even have understood that he was gone. Of course, I was very upset and confused by my father's death, and I knew my life was changing forever—but he had been my mother's husband, and it was she, not I, who would hereafter be called "widow."

There is no special name for adults who have lost one parent. They are still someone's child.

But when my mother died, for the first time in my life I could no longer find a way to protect myself from the full impact of loss. My sister had also lost her second parent, and that deserved attention. My children had lost their grandmother, and that deserved attention. Old family friends had lost another of their dwindling group, and that deserved attention. But I couldn't make the experience be about them.

In my heart and in my mind, my mother's death belonged to me. I was left without parents, and there was a name for that. I was an orphan. I had been overtaken by my lifelong nightmare, and the grief devoured me.

For the next few years, I was on an emotional roller coaster, ricocheting between feeling confused, lost, angry, sad, relieved, and numb—sometimes one at a time, sometimes all at once. My mood shifted from distracted to inconsolable and back in a heartbeat, without any discernible provocation. I would become upset over some small detail that in the past I would not even have noticed, and then I couldn't stop thinking about it. I was gloomy for a long time.

And I was afraid—just exactly as, years before, I had been afraid to go to sleep lest I awaken and find my parents gone. But this was no longer some vague dread of childhood. This was really happening. Every morning I awoke, and they were still gone.

It isn't that parental death is the most tragic loss we can suffer. It often isn't. The loss of a child, sibling, or spouse can be much more emotionally devastating.

It's not even that parental death is necessarily our first encounter with the death of a loved one. Many of us lose grandparents, family friends, even children, siblings, or spouses before our parents die.

I think it is the fulfillment of this most primal fear that makes parental death so profound. And it is the gradual realization that we will survive the loss that makes parental death so transforming.

After we recover (and, hard as it is to imagine at the time, we do recover), our life and reaction to death is changed. The power of our childhood dread of abandonment is vanquished—not because we are no longer afraid of death or because we no longer fear abandonment. That's not it.

It's that we have learned a lesson: We can transcend the enormity of loss, even our most feared loss, by grieving and growing larger ourselves.

From then on, whenever someone we know dies, we are more comfortable sitting with survivors—we may even want to. We might say the same things as before. We might do the same things as before. We may even be as afraid as we were before. But it isn't the same, because we are not the same. We have prevailed, and thereafter, we need to participate.

In the past we showed up because it was the right thing to and because we hoped it would be helpful. We now share in the common experience of vulnerability, sorrow, and confusion in the face of death that affirms our membership in the human community.

That capacity—to willingly go where we are afraid to go and find a bit of ourselves there—is courage. Courage generalizes, and it serves us well in our careers, our interpersonal relationships, and all other aspects of our lives. It makes it possible for us to make the hard choices that life presents and, often even harder, to face the consequences of the choices we have made.

We need courage, a lot of courage, to navigate the uncharted part of life after our parents die, the part that, on the maps of antiquity, were drawn as borders of dragons and serpents to warn of the fearsome dangers that always seem to lurk in the unknown.

The Map

Most of us don't actually get to know our parents very personally. They are always Mom and Dad. We are always "the kids." There is a barrier between generations, which, at least in part, is a function of the differences in our ages. However old our parents were when we were born, that is how much older than us they remain. Whether they are twenty, thirty, forty, or even fifty years ahead of us, they are always in a significantly different part of their lives than we are in ours.

They are already adults and parents, their youth available to us only through old photos and oft-told stories, when we are children. They are middle-aged, established at work, maybe even thinking about retirement when we enter the work world and begin to take our place as young adults.

They become grandparents—another role about which we know nothing—if we become parents. We may begin to comprehend some of the burdens and stressors with which they contended when first becoming parents themselves, but we still know little about what is going on for them at the time.

We are losing our grandparents when their parents are dying. We still have living parents and cannot understand that they are becoming orphans. We enter our prime working years when they are retiring. Our world is expanding and our friendships flourishing when they start to confront their own declining health, the deaths of their friends, and their shrinking worlds.

When they are discovering the form their deaths will take, we are learning about the nature of our grief as we watch them die.

After they are gone, we start to catch up. Each year, the gap between our age and the final age they attained diminishes. We begin to encounter events in life we saw them live through but, lacking a shared experience base, could not have understood. Gradually, we accumulate enough life experience to know, or at least to wonder in a more meaningful way, who they were.

I have a photograph that was taken of my parents and me on the day I was leaving for college. At the time, I was excited and a bit apprehensive, completely unaware that anything might be going on for them. For years, before my own youngest went off to college, I would look at that picture, and I would see my expression, and I could remember the complex emotions I was feeling at the time.

Now when I look at that picture, my attention is drawn to my mother's face, her unusual smile, and her sorrowful eyes. I can only imagine what was going on for her that day. Was she worried about how things would be for me so far from home? Was she worried about how things would be for her alone at home without children? Was she imagining how nice it would be to be rid of adolescent clutter? Was she remembering her own departure from her home as a young woman?

I cannot know. But I now wonder.

After our parents die, their time with us is sealed. Their lives are fully formed—with a beginning, a middle, and an end. Their story is complete and ready for the knowing. We can review their lives and begin recognizing the countless ways in which it is relevant to our own. Our lives continue: We move into and through our own middle age, evaluating our effectiveness and success in careers and relationships; we may begin to consider retiring; we may become grandparents; our health, and the health of our friends, may begin to ebb.

We may identify various qualities of our parents emerging in ourselves, perhaps in our mannerisms and attitudes, certainly in our reflections in the mirror.

Which is not to say that we necessarily become like them. Our behaviors may become more similar to theirs or more different, over time. Their conduct may become more understandable to us or less so. We may begin to better appreciate their lives or find them even more puzzling. But in the comparison, we begin to more fully comprehend and embrace our own behaviors, our own attitudes, and our own lives.

Many people who were treated cruelly by parents have told me that their parents' behavior toward them has become even more incomprehensible since their death. "I always figured they just saw things differently than I did because they were so much older," one woman told me. "But now that I'm that old, I really can't understand why they were so mean. My life is much harder in a lot of ways than theirs was, and I have kids now who are about the age I was then. It would never occur to me to use the harsh language with my boys that they used on me."

By contrast, another told me, "I used to think he was too strict with us when we were kids, but now I see the value of all those rules my dad made us live by."

And in those types of comparisons, we gradually locate ourselves. From countless contrasts and similarities, we begin to sketch beyond the edges of our original personal maps. It's how we find ourselves and how we continue finding our way on this journey through our lives.

None of us remembers agreeing to go on a journey in the first place. None of us knows where or how our stories will unfold. But we know we had parents. Our journey begins with, and for a long time overlaps, their map. After they die, we can find some of the rest of our map by studying the one they left behind. We evaluate some of their pathways and shortcuts, choosing which ones to follow, which ones to avoid.

So maybe part of the lesson we learn when parents die is in the study of maps: how to draw them, how to interpret them, how to know where we have been, where we are, and where else there is to go.

The Big Picture

While our parents are alive, reality occurs sequentially. Time moves in a straight line—past, present, future. It is as though we are passing through life on a train. Reality is what we are going through at the moment. It passes our window, real for as long as it is framed in our view. We might look out and see a pond, a bridge, a trestle, a wheat field, a town—all in view until we move on, and then, it becomes a memory.

We go to grade school. We learn the rules, do the assignments. This is our world. Then grade school is over, and we are ready for whatever's next. It becomes part of the past—a memory. The train has moved on.

We know that others were in grade school before we were, but that is the past—not *our* reality. We know that others will attend grade school after we leave, but that is in the future. It has no meaning to us. What is real is what is happening now.

There is a car for each generation on that train—our siblings, cousins, and friends are with us in one car; our parents, aunts, and uncles in the car ahead; maybe a grandparent car even farther ahead; eventually perhaps a car of children behind our own. All of us lined up in a row.

What goes on in our parents' car pertains to the middle-aged. What goes on in our grandparents' car pertains to the elderly. None of it pertains to us. They have their own train cars, their own problems, and their own stories. The old have always been old, the middle-aged always middle-aged, and we are forever young.

Our view of what is ahead is blocked by that parental car in front of us. We can only gaze through the side windows, through which reality scrolls past, a flat, two-dimensional picture—endless, and safe.

Then our parents die. The car ahead of ours is gone. For the first time, we can see out the front. Life, reality, and time look dramatically different in the bright light of this new panorama. It may be all we can do, at first, just to not avert our eyes to avoid the harshness of that unfamiliar glare. The view now includes the future, and it is not endless.

We see, and start to know, to *really* know—not just know with our minds, but know with our skin, our cells, and our souls—that we are now in the lead car. We are next in line.

Without the protective illusion of our parents' timeless presence, the future begins to have urgent meaning. We may begin to cling to the past for support because it is filled with precious memories that contain our roots, and, we discover, they're what is holding us up. The former distinctions between past, present, and future begin to blur.

We may introduce our past to the future by beginning to tell stories about our childhood, and the stories our parents told us about their childhood, to our children. We may introduce the past to the present by displaying photographs of ancestors we used to think of as father's family or mother's family but now think of as "our" family. We may blend the present with the future by planning our legacy, writing a will, doing estate planning, buying more life insurance. We may stop putting vacations and other things we always wanted to do off until the future. We may begin to realize that the future, the past, and the present are all the same.

Reality is no longer an orderly sequence from the past through the present to the future that scrolls past the window of a train. And we are not just passengers.

Reality, it turns out, is much more complex, much richer, than that—and this is the most precious lesson we can learn after our parents die.

Approximately a year before my mother died, I found a picture of her and her sisters that was taken when they were little girls in a ballet class in Moscow. I thought it a lovely picture of a scene from my mother's past, so I got it framed and hung it up in our house. That's what it was to me at the time—a lovely picture from my mother's past.

After my mother died, I looked at that picture again, and it had become something completely different to me: I, already much older than the girl in the photograph, could look at that smiling young face and see my mother—and my daughter. At the same time, I could remember the charming lady I think of when I think of my mom. I could feel sorrow about the pitiful old helpless woman my mother became in the last years of her life. I could ache, and know I would always ache, from the eternal absence she left behind when she died. Past, present, and future were all the same now. All at the same time. All part of my reality.

It's everywhere I look. I am simultaneously the baby whose picture is in the old family album, the boy of my childhood memories, the middle-aged man I am today, and the feeble old man I will someday become. My children are still the infants I once held in one arm at the same time that they are the parents of my grandchildren. My great-grandfather, whose photograph hangs in our house, looks at us from out of his frame, his eye occasionally catching mine. I never knew him and I will never know my great grandchildren, but in a way, I already know them both. In a way, I am them both.

Gaining this perspective permits us to more broadly define ourselves and to participate more fully in life. The concerns of the old are our concerns because that's where we are heading. The concerns of the young are our concerns as well because we are forever connected to youth.

Life, we discover, is so much more involved and amazing than what we can see out of a train window. More, even, than the view out the front and back.

In fact, it is no longer as though we are passengers looking out the window of a speeding train, at all. We are the engine, the caboose, and all the cars in between, clickety-clacking along the tracks that stretch, sparkling in the sun, all the way to the horizon.

We are the tracks. We are the rocky path along which those tracks meander, the tiny weeds growing along the edges, the countryside of rolling hills, and the infinite sky above in endless shades of blue.